Working with Oneness

Working with Oneness

LLEWELLYN VAUGHAN-LEE

First published in the United States in 2002 by
The Golden Sufi Center
P.O. Box 428, Inverness, California 94937.

© 2002 by The Golden Sufi Center.

Printed and bound by Thomson-Shore, Inc.

Library of Congress Cataloging-in-Publication Data

Vaughan-Lee, Llewellyn.
  Working with oneness / Llewellyn Vaughan-Lee.
      p. ; cm.
Includes bibliographical references and index.
  ISBN 1-890350-05-2 (alk. paper)
  1. Spiritual life. I. Title.
  BL624 .V3865 2002
  291.4'4--dc21

                              2002018830

Cover art acknowledgments: The Tate Gallery, for permission to use Cecil
Collins' image *Bird Singing in a Tree*, ink and pencil on white paper (1944);
and NSSDC for supplying the data for the image of the sun eclipse.

CONTENTS

God has shouted 'Yes! Yes! Yes!'
To every luminous movement in Existence.

Hafiz

In each mirror, each moment
A new face reveals His beauty.

Fakhruddîn 'Irâqî

PREFACE

Throughout this book, in an effort to maintain continuity and simplicity of text, God, the Great Beloved, is referred to as He. Of course, the Absolute Truth is neither masculine nor feminine. As much as It has a divine masculine side, so It has an awe-inspiring feminine aspect.

Introduction

THE ENERGY OF THE NEW AGE

I am by nature a spiritual traditionalist. My journey has taken me down the ancient path of the mystic, and although it has been a solitary journey, from the alone to the Alone, I have walked in the footsteps of those who have gone before. In the writings of the Sufi masters I have found guidance and reassurance, knowing that they have mapped out the stages of the heart, the mystery of the heart's awakening to the divine presence. "New Age" spiritual teachings held little interest for me. Therefore, I was surprised to find in January 2000 a new energy arriving unannounced, an energy that carried with it promises and ideals that extended beyond my own spiritual horizons.

At first I thought that this energy was just the next step on my own journey. But it soon made known to me that it was not personal, but belonged to a whole new beginning. With power and speed it swept away years of spiritual conditioning, and brought with it a quality of fun and pure joy that I knew I had always been waiting for. Mercilessly, laughingly, it began to change my life, my way of thinking, my way of relating. This energy is alive, demanding change and needing to be lived in the midst of life. And it has a quality of oneness that brings with it a stamp of divine presence.

A few months after this energy awoke me with its demanding intensity, I visited an old friend in London, a seventy-year-old woman whose clarity, humor, and down-to-earth spiritual wisdom I have long valued. I told her about this energy, and she said that she had also experienced it, and seen the effect it had on people in her meditation group: how it brought things to the light which had long been kept hidden, and had a clear, impersonal quality. Then I began to see this energy arriving in the dreams and visions of other friends, expressing a new image of divine oneness that is now alive in the world. One friend had a dream in which she was part of a membrane of light and love that covered the whole world. Another friend dreamed of the earth, "and around the earth is a beautiful web of light, and everything is in movement, like little stars and suns. I was fascinated by the harmony within everything—so much light and movement and so few collisions."

One friend had a vision in which he saw "a gigantic, golden grid composed of either circles or octagons, each circle perfectly melded into the next. I knew that this had just come into being, as a whole, or as a part of a whole. It had just been created, and was awesomely powerful."

And another friend describes a similar picture she was shown in meditation: "I saw a nearly round golden net against a total blackness. It was made of extremely fine golden wire, and the threads which went to the center were at some points folded or bent into Arabic writing which I could not read. But somehow I knew that it had to do with the aspects of God. The center was an empty circle or octagon. The threads which crossed the 'spokes' were without writing. Only the 'spokes' carried the aspects."

These dreams and visions all carry a quality of light and wholeness, and an energy that is alive with the oneness of divine presence. And they have the sense of something coming into being, arriving at the threshold of consciousness. Mystics have always worked at the threshold of consciousness, where new life comes from the unformed and uncreated into manifestation. Lovers are familiar with the unknowable vastness, the infinite ocean from where love flows into the world. It is here, at the borders of the beyond, that changes first take place, and it is here that this new energy is now dynamically alive, flowing down into creation.

This energy brings with it the promise of a new future, a future born not from the past but from the eternal moment. And it carries the joy of life, unpolluted and unconditioned. It is impersonal and powerful, and needs to be lived. Only through being lived can it be brought into the world. It requires our full attention and participation; otherwise its promise will not come to fruition. It is very fluid and organic, and has the capacity to change very rapidly, to adapt itself while staying true to its essential nature. And yet because it has not yet reached the plane of manifestation, it has little form, is hardly visible.

Everything that is created comes from the inner worlds. The energy of life flows from the uncreated emptiness out into the planes of manifestation. This is why events first constellate on the inner planes. As the energy of life comes into manifestation, it becomes more visible. At first it takes form as a pattern of energy, a fluid, dynamically flowing reality out of which the primal oneness of creation begins to differentiate itself. This is the archetypal dimension where undifferentiated energy constellates into the forms behind the physical world. Finally the energy of creation enters the physical plane and becomes part of the world of the senses, at which time it becomes fixed into matter, into a physical form or event. Once energy becomes embodied, takes form on the physical plane, it is fixed and more difficult to work with; it requires more effort to change. On the inner planes one can move energy through conscious attention, while on the physical plane change often involves laborious effort.

WORKING WITH WHAT IS UNDEFINED

This new energy demands our attention and our participation, yet it is hardly visible, glimpsed mostly in dreams and visions. How can we work with what we do not know, what we cannot see? First we need to know that this energy is present, and that although it is invisible, our consciousness can become attuned to it. Like subatomic particles, which are visible only through their effects, this energy can become known through its signs, the way it interacts with us.

The energy of oneness dynamically moves, interacts, and constellates in a new way. This book offers some guidance about how to work with it and the attitude that is required for this work. Because this energy is new and undefined, there are no fixed rules, and yet it has certain qualities that will define the nature of our participation with it. For example, it is so new that we ourselves must be as free as possible of our personal and collective conditioning in order to work with it. Also, this energy has an impersonal nature and a global dimension that require that we shift our focus away from our own individual inner journey and give ourself to the work of the whole. And it is an energy of life itself, and so it demands that we live it in all aspects of our ordinary, everyday existence.

This energy and the patterns through which it comes into creation cannot be defined or described with any exactness. Instead they require a new way of relating to life, of interacting with life as an energy flow rather than something fixed or static. If you try to grasp it as a defined concept you will be frustrated, because it is too fluid and alive to be made concrete. As with flowing water, the moment you hold it, its essential quality of motion disappears. Yet through observing its movement we can come to know some of its qualities, how it flows, how it carries things along. The energy patterns of life are very dynamic, but if they are met with an attitude of receptivity and attention they can reveal to us their nature and how to work with them.

This is a time of wonderful opportunity because we have the capacity to create our own destiny, to work directly with the energy of life as it comes into being. We may have to renounce our spiritual expectations and leave behind many patterns of conditioning. But there is a celebration waiting to be lived and we are being asked to participate. This shift is so fundamental that it requires courage and a sense of adventure. We do not know what will happen and yet we are standing on the edge of a new age that has arrived so completely we have barely noticed it.

The danger is always to try to make something concrete and defined, to look for clear advice or an exact path to follow. But the mystic who swims in love's infinite ocean knows that nothing real can be defined, it can only be glimpsed or hinted at. We need both common sense and a commitment to what is new. We have to live the reality of what is here as well as the infinite possibilities of the future. This energy will affect us each in our own way, and will often go undetected because it is so new. We always look for what we know, for the way our conditioning has prepared us. What is wondrous and unexpected takes longer to accustom ourselves to. Nor do we realize the degree to which our intention, our attitude, our individual participation can affect the life of the whole and the way the future will unfold. At the dusk of a patriarchal era, we are still conditioned to being children who are told what to do.

The future is here and waiting to be lived, and it carries the stamp of divine oneness. The energy that is needed to change everything has arrived, and although it has not yet come into manifestation, we can work with it. The energy of divine oneness is not separate from us, and individual consciousness has the capacity to become directly attuned to it. Through conscious attention we can work with this energy as it comes into manifestation. One of its qualities is that it carries within it the knowledge that is needed in order to work with it. This knowledge is also fluid, organic, relating directly to "the need of the time and the place and the people." This is why the first task of the future is to learn how to be attentive and responsive. The knowledge of the future is too dynamic and too responsive to the changing conditions of the moment to be fixed. It is given freely, and only requires that we give it our undivided attention, that we say "yes" to the now. Through our conscious participation this knowledge is revealed to us; it comes alive through us. We are needed to help this energy come into being, to bring it alive in our world. Without our conscious cooperation the future will not be born in its full potential. We are the book in which the knowledge of oneness is being written.

Global Energy Patterns

Look close: all is He—
But He is manifest through me.

Fakhruddîn 'Irâqî[1]

THE PLANET AS AN ENERGY STRUCTURE

The energy structure of the planet is changing. It is becoming more dynamic and fluid, more visible and accessible. Humanity is now being given the opportunity to relate directly with this energy structure and participate in a shift from a consciousness defined through separation and differentiation to a consciousness of oneness. This is the next step in our evolution, and it will influence every level of life on this planet.

Energy underlies all life, flows in certain patterns, along specific paths, affecting and connecting matter and consciousness alike. How and where energy flows in part determines how life manifests in this world. As the energy patterns of the planet change, so too will the patterns and possibilities of creation.

The spiritual transformation of an individual awakens new centers of energy for that person. The same is true of the whole of humanity and the planet. At each stage of evolution humanity is given more access to the energy of the planet. In the past few centuries we have focused on the physical energy of fossil fuels, and work with this energy has dominated our social development. But this focus on the physical is now shifting and we are being given access to a different level of energy.

The new energy that is becoming available to us is an energy of oneness that can help us live our true role in relation to the planet, a role of stewardship based on conscious interconnectedness. Changes in the energy structure of the planet and the availability of this new energy of oneness are aspects of the next stage in our collective and individual evolution, a stage that allows a shift from isolation and separation into oneness and communion with all creation.

In order to take this step we must abandon our conditioned ways of perceiving and relating to matter, and acknowledge the existence of these energy patterns that form part of the underlying structure of life. We have to stop experiencing the world as a purely physical entity, separate and distinct from ourselves, and relate to it as a flow of energy that by its nature includes us. Particle physics asserts an image of matter as a dynamic energy field, a dancing flow of energy patterns that coalesce into physical form. If we accept this image of matter we will be freed from a static, defined world in which only material objects have substance, and be drawn into a more fluid, dynamic, and inclusive relationship with life.

Our culture has not yet stepped into this paradigm. We still regard life as composed of dense material objects rather than an interflow of energy. We are still living in a nineteenth-century universe, rather than embracing the consciousness offered by our own scientific revolution. The science that drew us out of the symbolic world of the Middle Ages has moved beyond the familiar image of a defined physical universe governed by Newtonian physics.

We continue to identify our planet as simply a physical sphere spinning in space, part of a solar system. But this is only the viewpoint posited by a science fathered by Galileo. We see the world through the glasses of scientific, rational materialism, not recognizing that this is just a projected image of our planet, an image that our science has already moved beyond. Other eras have perceived the world through different glasses: as a living, sacred being, our mother the earth, or as a part of a symbolic universe in which mankind played its central role in the "great chain of being." As cultures change and evolve, so they offer a different perspective on life and the planet.

We can hardly begin to imagine the possibilities born from a shift away from a materialistic view of reality to a more dynamic understanding of life as energy. But if we look around us we can see signs that we are beginning to recognize and relate to life through the energy patterns that underlie it.

The internet and other means of global communication are examples. Opportunities for global communication and information exchange are increasing at this time in part due to our growing capacity to align our individual consciousness with the patterns of energy that flow throughout the planet. Global communication is in itself the activation of a global energy pattern. Additionally, multinational corporations are unknowingly accessing energy patterns and using them to increase the range and speed of their businesses. In Joseph Campbell's words, "money is congealed energy," and the way the global flow of money enables material goods to move around the world at greatest profit is a direct use of global energy patterns.

Because these energy patterns are most accessible in the midst of life, people working in business and commerce unknowingly have the most immediate access to them. Also, successful businessmen often have an intuitive understanding of how money works, how it flows and constellates. They can instinctively tune into and utilize the way the energy of money follows global energy patterns. The use of computers and the internet to as-similate and move information as well as money in an ever-expanding network is also increasing the potency of corporations and their ability to tap into these un-derlying energy patterns. The possibilities for personal gain are enormous, and this is what drives most new ventures.

However, the higher purpose of giving human be-ings conscious access to the energy structure of the plan-et is not to produce global corporations of vast wealth and power. Having money, power, and physical resources in the control of a few individuals or corporations (how-ever "global") works against the very nature of the flow of energy, which needs to be continually moving rather than be caught in any fixed configuration. If the energy structure becomes static or crystallized, then the possi-bilities for new life cease.

FRIENDS OF GOD

Since the very beginning of humanity there have been spiritual masters who have kept watch on the world and for the world. These masters and their disciples have worked to keep humanity aligned with the currents of energy, of love and wisdom, that come from the inner planes. These masters also work to keep the energy flow-ing and balanced, in accordance with the need of the time and the laws of the inner world. In the Sufi tradi-tion there is a spiritual hierarchy of the *awliyâ* (Friends of God), which consists of a fixed number of evolved beings, without whom the existence and well-being of the world cannot be maintained. At the top of the hierarchy stands the *pole (qutb)*, "the Master of the Friends of God," who is the axis around whom the exterior and interior universe turns. Under the *pole* come seven *pegs*, below which come the forty *successors (al-abdâl)*.[2] If one of these Friends of God dies another is waiting to take his place, so that the number is maintained.[3]

Traditionally the Friends of God work in hiding, veiled from the world. This enables them to continue their work without the disturbance that recognition could bring. Ibn 'Arabî, the great thirteenth-century Sufi master, tells the story of when he was in Fez. There he met a Sufi called al-Ashall (literally "the withered" because he had a withered hand). Ibn 'Arabî had been in his company a number of times without knowing his spiritual station, until he had a vision in which it was revealed to him that al-Ashall was the *pole* of the time. The next day he was invited to someone's garden to meet with a group of Sufis, among them al-Ashall. Nobody talked to this man, who was a foreigner. But during the conversation the *pole* came to be mentioned, and Ibn 'Arabî said, "'My brothers I am going to tell you some amazing things about the *pole* of your time." He then turned towards the man who during his sleep had been shown to him by God to be the *pole*.... This man said to Ibn 'Arabî, "Say what God has revealed to you, but do not reveal his identity!'"[4]

The Friends of God have been working with the energy structure of the planet for centuries, but have kept this knowledge hidden, as it could easily be misused. These masters of love and wisdom are now working to help humanity align with the changes that are currently taking place, changes that begin first on the inner planes before they come into manifestation. Energy patterns are becoming accessible to consciousness, and humanity needs to know how to use this energy for spiritual benefit rather than just material gain.

In the past few decades spiritual teachings that used to be known only to initiates have been given to the world. This has helped to create an environment receptive to the changes that are about to take place. Many sincere spiritual practitioners have used this knowledge to work on themselves and thus become inwardly receptive to what is being given. Many spiritual techniques that have been made available are essentially a process of purification that helps the individual become aligned with her true nature. This is a necessary first step in the process of spiritual awakening. We need to be aligned with our real Self in order to manifest the higher destiny that belongs to the soul. The real work begins only when we are aligned with our essential nature, because it is only then that the higher energies of the inner world can manifest without being distorted.[5]

Those who have made the step away from their ego-self into the faster-spinning vortex of their real Self are now needed to work for humanity. The work that needs to be done cannot be performed by just the few Friends of God and their disciples. The forces of materialism are so powerful and dense that on their own, the masters of wisdom cannot pierce through. They need the help of all those who carry a commitment to humanity within their hearts. The inner wisdom of the Self, a wisdom of love and unity, needs to be brought down to a lower plane of manifestation. This requires a collective spiritual effort.

ACCESS TO KNOWLEDGE

In the past an individual had to go through many levels of initiation before he was allowed to help with the spiritual work for humanity. The training was long and arduous, and many failed to reach the required degree of purity and selflessness. Although no one was excluded, many slipped by the wayside, and their path remained within the sphere of individual development. This has changed. Instructions have been given by those who look after the destiny of humanity to allow anyone who is sincere to have access to the secrets of initiation, to be given an understanding of the energy structure of the world, in order to help in this time of transition.

Of course there is the danger that this knowledge will be misused, that even sincere seekers will be misled by the subtle intrigues of the ego and its desires. This does not matter. This danger has already been taken into account by those who look out for humanity. We are being given the opportunity to take the next step in our development as human beings, to take more responsibility for ourself and our planet.

True spiritual work is always an individual effort, and this will not change. Just as true maturity is an individual step, so is spiritual evolution. Only as individuals standing on our own feet can we make a valid contribution to the collective. Otherwise we remain caught in the collective and its patterns of co-dependency that block any real change or development. Taking responsibility for our inner and outer life is necessary if we are to participate creatively in the life of the whole.

The knowledge that is being made available will necessarily confront us with our own inadequacies and a pull to retreat into the familiar patterns of the past. For example, many spiritual seekers are identified with the notion of a spiritual journey that needs to be completed, an inner work that needs to be accomplished. It is not easy to step aside from such long-held beliefs, particularly those that engender spiritual well-being. Those spiritual practitioners who have achieved some degree of spiritual position which supports them will have the most to lose. The spiritual security that comes from having been on a path or engaged in spiritual activities for a number of years can also be a hindrance to change.

Christ tells a story about the owner of a vineyard who went out in the early morning to hire some men, agreeing to pay them a penny for a day's work. Then three hours later the owner went to the marketplace and hired some more men, offering to pay them what was right. He did the same at noon and at three in the afternoon. Then, an hour before sunset, he went again to the marketplace, and finding others idle, offered them work in his vineyard. At the end of the day he told his steward to pay each man a penny for his work, beginning with those who were hired last. When each was paid a penny, those who had worked from the early morning complained that those who had just been working one hour before sunset were paid the same as those who had worked all day. But the owner answered, saying that he had given them what he had promised. They should take their penny and go, and he would give to the last the same as to the first.[6]

Each of those who works in the vineyard of the Lord is given a penny, a symbol of his own wholeness. This is the gift for spiritual work: we are given ourselves. It is given to all those who participate. Those who have worked since dawn and "borne the heat and burden of the day" may complain, but they do not understand that to participate in the work of the whole for even an instant is to be given access to one's own wholeness. This is the experience that is now being offered to all who are drawn into the sphere of spiritual life. As a culture we are so identified with patterns of hierarchy and their levels of exclusion that we overlook the primary truth that the dimension of oneness is all-inclusive. The moment we turn our focus away from our own ego-self and participate in the work of the whole, we step into the circle of our own wholeness. There are no levels of initiation: one is either in or out. And someone who has just begun on the path is given as much access as someone who has been engaged in spiritual practice for many years.

THE GIFT OF WHOLENESS

Human beings have a deep hunger to regain a conscious connection with their own wholeness. We are collectively tired of the forces that isolate us within our ego-oriented life, that offer us only a fragmented sense of our self. We long to regain our wholeness and natural sense of being. And yet as a culture we seem to have lost our way. As we move faster and faster down the track of self-absorption, we encounter more feelings of inadequacy. We have lost touch with the simplicity of being and sadly look to material wealth to fill this void. Even spiritual seekers are only too often preoccupied with achieving, developing, becoming something other than what they are. With more and more effort we chase the illusive image of what we think we need.

Wholeness is always present. If we do not know that our own wholeness is present, we won't recognize it or open to it when it is offered. Wholeness can be difficult to recognize because it is complete; it does not function through comparison, through the opposition of light and dark. It is difficult to recognize wholeness through our ordinary modes of perception, by defining it against what it is not.

Wholeness is so lacking in all the attributes of success and achievement that we do not value it. It is so completely different from the hierarchical power structures that have dominated our collective landscape for so long that we do not know how to assess it. It does not play power games or try to achieve anything. And wholeness does not give position or preference. Nobody is higher up the ladder, whether this ladder is of worldly success or spiritual achievement. Rather each person is complete in herself, and in her natural sense of completeness is able to participate fully in the life of the whole.

Just to recognize that this wholeness is present is the first step; then we must realize that it is given, that we do not have to achieve it. The only requirement is to leave behind the patterns of conditioning that tie us to hierarchical models of achievement and failure. This is done by admitting that we are tired of this model, tired of the demands of success, exhausted by the struggles of failure. We are so conditioned by the idea that we have to struggle for what we want that it can be revolutionary to realize that we are being given something that only requires our acceptance and participation.

Before, we had to work to regain our wholeness: we had to turn inward, meditate, purify ourselves, do battle with the ego and patterns of conditioning. Now our wholeness is being given to us without restriction. No initiation is needed; there are no levels to be achieved. A quality of oneness is being made freely available to humanity. We just have to accept the gift.

What had been hidden within us, accessible only to those who made the inner journey, is now being made visible. The oneness that is our essential nature is being revealed. The work of those committed in service is to make this known so people can recognize what they are being given and make use of this opportunity. We need to know that a consciousness of oneness is present, not as a distant promise or an abstract idea, but as a reality that exists within and around us. What had been a secret, accessible only to initiates, is being made available to everyone.

The internet is a relatively new model of universal consciousness in which knowledge, or information, is readily available to anyone, anywhere. All that is required is a computer and a connection and one has instant access to a unified body of knowledge and the potential for interconnecting with everyone else who is on the internet. The unified connectivity presented by the internet has been long known to the mystic, who in meditation has access to a dimension of oneness in which everything is simultaneously present, and all knowledge is accessible. The experience of *samadhi*, or superconscious state, happens on this plane of oneness. But the internet presents a model of a unified consciousness that is accessible on a more physical plane, to anyone who has access to a computer.

The internet is at present only in its infancy, but it carries the blueprint of its potential—a consciousness of global oneness and interrelationship that defies the barriers of nationality and geography. It is present everywhere at the same time. The internet is not a hierarchical structure, and despite the desire of some companies or governments to control it, it is globally democratic. At the present time it is primarily used for accessing information and communication. But it has the potential to create patterns of interrelationship that will form the network for a global unity and consciousness. The flow of information through an expanded web of individual relationships throughout the planet will be like a cellular structure that comes alive and continually makes new connections. As these connections of both knowledge and people become activated, they will make further connections in a way that is very similar to how the brain activates and accesses information. At a critical point the interrelationships and flow of information come alive and begin to function as a unified field—a unified level of consciousness on a global level is activated.

As we stand at the beginning of this new era, we can use the tools and opportunities that are being given to further our material domination of the planet and our own ego-driven desires. Those who have the more direct access to these tools and understand their potential have the possibility of becoming immensely wealthy— wealthy on a global scale. Alternatively, we can step aside from these patterns of the past that are based upon competition and domination and begin to recognize the real potential of what we are being given. We can use our access to oneness for a higher rather than lower purpose. We can enable something to be given to the whole of humanity, and also to the planet of which we are the guardians. We can help the seeds of oneness reveal their real potential, to flourish and grow, and so enable certain fundamental changes to take place to the whole of life.

TRANSITION AND GLOBAL IMBALANCE

Oneness is very simple: everything is included and allowed to live according to its true nature. This is the secret that is being revealed, the opportunity that is offered. How we make use of this opportunity depends upon the degree of our participation, how much we are prepared to give ourselves to the work that needs to be done, to the freedom that needs to be lived. The opportunity is everywhere at the same time, because this is the nature of oneness. And it is totally individual, because it respects the divine oneness that is present within each atom of creation, embodied in every human being. Human beings have the unique capacity to live this oneness consciously, to know and live their own uniqueness, their own participation in the whole. This is His gift to humanity, and with this gift comes also the free will that allows us to make mistakes, to miss the opportunity that is being given.

We are capable of continuing with the same ego-oriented goals that have dominated our cultures for centuries and of using the tools of oneness to further these aims. Then the power structures that have access to these tools will become very powerful on a global scale and a certain imbalance will become irreversible. Finally these power structures will self-destruct as they are not meant to continue into the next millennium. But their destruction could be catastrophic and cause much pain and suffering. Humanity would then have to rebuild itself from the debris of the past. This has happened before many times—one has only to remember the destruction caused by the Third Reich in the last century. Or looking back further, the Dark Ages in Europe that followed the downfall of the Roman Empire, an empire that had become unbalanced and corrupted with power. However, as the present power structures become global, it is likely that their downfall will have a global effect, rather than being contained within a country or continent. Chaos on a global scale is a very real possibility—and the ecological state of the planet offers visible warnings of this.

But there is also the possibility that this transition to a new era can be made without a global disaster. If enough people access the new energy of oneness over the next few years and learn to use it according to its higher potential, then there can be healing rather than destruction. How this will happen is not yet known, except that people and groups are being positioned throughout the planet to create a container of energy that will minimize the destructive effects of this transition. They are creating a cocoon of love and power that can help humanity where the need is greatest. Every time of transition is dangerous as well as full of potential. We need to know that we are supported and contained, that we are being helped. We need to know that the Friends of God and their helpers are with us, guiding us, directing the currents of love and wisdom as they have done for millennia.

THE CONSCIOUSNESS OF HUMANITY

If it is used creatively and for the purpose of the whole, the energy of oneness can have a healing and beneficial effect. The energy of oneness activates our own latent wholeness, and this can happen on an individual and planetary scale. In fact, if we realize wholeness within ourselves we also realize it within the planet, because we are far more interconnected with the energy structure of the planet than we know. Through our own participation with the energy of oneness we can help the planet align with its own wholeness. We can help bring the healing and transformative energy of oneness into life where it can redeem what has been polluted by our materialism and greed.

Recognizing our own wholeness and the interrelated wholeness of all life is the first step in this work. One of the most important contributions of the ecological movement is that it has made us conscious of the interdependence of all forms of life, the delicate web of creation. Ecology has also given us a heightened awareness of our stewardship of the planet. Our capacity for consciousness makes us responsible not only for our individual self but also for our planet. And yet we are reluctant to take this step, to grow out of our self-absorbed adolescence into the responsibilities of adulthood. Part of our childishness is that we are always waiting for someone else to save us, instead of fully accepting responsibility for ourselves and our planet.

We are an integral part of life, and we hold the seeds of change in our consciousness. The consciousness of humanity *is* the consciousness of the planet; we carry the consciousness of the world within us. Just as the divine evolves through man, so does the planet evolve through the activity and attitude of humanity. The world is not simply a physical place to support and nourish us, to give us what we want. If we continue to relate to the planet with this attitude, it, in turn, will relate to us as goods for sale, goods that will eventually be depleted. Rather, we are guardians of the planet and the whole of life. We are being given the tools and opportunities to help us accept our role more consciously, to interact more responsibly with the evolution of the whole.

Once we accept that everything we need is already present, we can work with the energy patterns of life as they are made known to us. At the moment they are still just at the borders of consciousness. They can be glimpsed but not defined. As we work with them they will become more accessible; to become visible, they need our consciousness. To take on form, they need the connections of our brain and the interconnections between people.

We carry the consciousness of the planet in our own consciousness and it is made known through us. These energy patterns are not separate from us. At the highest level they have the substance of our divine consciousness, our relationship to God. At the lowest level they are reflected in how money and goods move around the world, how our mechanisms for physical survival and well-being function. But in this time of transition they are very fluid. That is why the possibilities for the future are being born now. It is through our conscious participation that these energy patterns will take on form and determine the life on our planet for centuries to come. The more we can be conscious of our divine potential in everyday life, the more these energy patterns will reflect and help to manifest our divine nature, and the more the imprint of His oneness will come alive. Once this energy fully hits the plane of manifestation, its patterns become imprinted into the substance of life and, like riverbeds, determine where life's energy flows.

Stepping into this role of adult responsibility, we move beyond our matriarchal identification as children supported by "our mother the earth," and the patriarchal image of being under the distant, watchful, and sometimes judgmental eye of "our father in heaven."[7] Instead we must embrace a totally new paradigm which will radically alter our relationship to the planet and to the divine. A consciously co-creative relationship with the energy of the planet and the divine that recognizes the oneness inherent in life will open the door to a new era of humanity, with possibilities for our individual and collective life that until now have only been a utopian dream.

If we step fully into this role, the energy flow of the planet will start to heal the planet. The planet will come alive in a new way, and offer us possibilities for life that are not yet accessible. Maturity brings with it both responsibility and new possibilities. We know this in our own journey into adulthood, how our horizon expands as we step out of the world of childhood. Mankind is a microcosm of the whole, and what happens within an individual can happen to the whole of humanity. We can begin to have access to more of our potential as human beings.

The Sufi knows that we are made in the image of God, and that as we grow we more fully awaken to our divine nature and its potential. The spiritual journey of the wayfarer takes us out of the limited horizon of the physical, temporal world, and our ego-self, into the circle of oneness and love. The divine nature of the human being contains possibilities for life that are beyond our imaginings. Spiritual knowledge points to our potential as human beings and it is time that we use this knowledge to enrich our lives, which have become dull and colorless through our focus on the material world. Central to our spiritual awareness is the consciousness of oneness, the experience of the divine oneness of life. Bringing this consciousness into everyday life has the potential to awaken humanity to its divine nature and help us to realize the real meaning of life on this planet, the true function of our stewardship.

Everyday Life

Tell me: if the hidden treasure is now on display
at the bazaar, shouldn't the gnostic leave his cell
and wander forth?

Gharib Nawâz[1]

THE FLOW OF LIFE AS AN ENERGY OF HEALING

As we come to view life as interrelating energy patterns, we will begin to awaken to the possibilities of the future. We will come to recognize the energy patterns that link different forms of life together, and see how life on this planet is an interdependent whole. We will see how each aspect of humanity dynamically interacts with the whole, how all the seemingly disparate races, cultures, and even individuals complement each other. For just as the ecological structure of life is a complex web of interdependent systems, so is the dynamic energy structure of the whole of humanity.

At the present time our focus on our individual and national identity creates a barrier that inhibits our consciousness from flowing globally. Just as we can block or deny ourself an experience of life with our individual patterns of thought and conditioning, we do the same with our collective thought-forms. We create a filter on the inner planes that determines our experience of life as a collective, which is then even more difficult to break through than our individual patterns since it is maintained and reinforced by group thought and behavior.

The awakening sense of a global horizon, brought about partly by the technological advances in communication, has the potential to dramatically alter our patterns of perception. Embracing a global consciousness draws us away from an isolationist, insular attitude. Consciousness itself is dramatically affected by a global perspective. A consciousness that looks to the whole is far more expansive and powerful than one caught within the fragmented image of an insular identity. If we look to the whole we are supported by the whole, just as if we only look to ourself we are only supported by ourself. A global consciousness gives us access to a different level of awareness and support. It also demands that we take responsibility for the whole.

The need for global responsibility is self-evident, yet this expanded responsibility directly confronts the forces of greed and ego-driven desire that have for so long dominated our individual and collective landscape. Here is where the battleground of the next decades is being drawn.

The visible power structures of the present, even those with a "global vision," are dominated mainly by the desires of material greed and personal power. Global corporations rarely have the well-being of the whole as their prime motivation, and are instead driven by profit incentive. We don't yet realize that using global energy systems for personal gain creates a dangerous imbalance—the energy does not flow freely. This will create even greater areas of deprivation than we presently experience. In order for us to take the next step in our evolution, we must not limit our global consciousness by desire for personal gain, but rather use it to help the energy of life flow unrestricted throughout an organic self-regenerating system.

If the energy of life can flow freely, life will naturally bring sustenance to where it is needed most. The whole can nourish and sustain itself in the best possible fashion—this is part of the dynamics of wholeness. Then the energy of the new millennium will find its way around the blocks that seem to limit our development. If enough people are prepared to participate, to work with the energy of the planet for the sake of the whole, the planet can awaken as a self-nurturing, self-healing, self-sustaining system.

This is the work that needs to be done. And there is an urgency. If the present power structures that use global energy patterns for individual gain become too powerful, they will be able to resist the dynamic of change in a way that will precipitate destruction. But if the energy is able to shift before this happens, then there can be a peaceful time of transition in which the present power structures will gradually lose their momentum, or be transformed into non-hierarchical organic organizations that can work for the benefit of the whole rather than the few.

IN THE MARKETPLACE

We are each being given the opportunity to participate in this time of transition according to our unique individual nature. We are being asked to say "yes" to who we really are and to live our essential nature for the purpose of the whole. Our limitation is our concern for our personal well-being, even our spiritual well-being. This is why any concern for spiritual progress has to be put to one side. The inner journey will continue, but will no longer be the focus of our efforts. Instead, we must all look towards everyday life as the means to live our deepest qualities.

The work of the soul is being manifested in a way that has not been allowed before. Mystics and spiritual seekers of all kinds are being called to participate in life in a way that until now has been denied them. Their spiritual qualities are needed to give a certain color to the marketplace, to give a certain frequency of energy to life. They are needed to make something happen—to awaken the heart of the world.

If the energy of spiritual transformation is brought into the marketplace of life, then life can respond. A certain energy can be released from within life that is needed for the evolution of the whole. Only those who have turned towards God can make this happen. This is their central contribution at this time of change. They hold the key for certain energy fields within life, certain doors that have not been opened before but need to be opened now. If this work is not done, then life will stagnate and a frequency of freedom will not be accessible to humanity.

There is no longer the time to focus on personal or even spiritual development. This focus turns us away from our global, collective responsibility and thus limits our participation in the work of the moment. We must give up our plans for enlightenment, even for absorption in God. We return to the source only to participate in life more fully. We give ourself to God only to be *here* for Him, to be able to be more fully engaged in His work for humanity. And nobody is better, or nearer, or further along this path, because it is our own individual relationship to life that matters: our unique ability to see His oneness reflected in His creation, to bring the oneness hidden within our heart out into life. We have been given what we need, and will be sustained by His love. We are each alone and yet we are all together, because we are here for His sake. We are supported by the Friends of God, and yet we each have to stand on our own feet. And the time is right now.

EMPTINESS AND THE FULLNESS OF LIFE

For so long we have separated ourselves from life. Even our spirituality has asked us to step aside. We have longed for a transcendence so total that we came to consider our existence here on earth unimportant. Our practice of surrender was to purify ourselves until nothing of us remained, until God acted through us as we watched from the side. We have been working to empty ourselves so something else can fill us, something else can come into the world.

But now we are asked to participate in a new way; we are asked to participate as ourselves, completely and fully engaging in life around us. Emptiness is no longer a goal, something to attain through purification, but a surrender lived through complete participation. Being used is no longer an aspiration, but the living potential of every moment. We don't have to wait to be used. Waiting until we are empty enough to be used denies God's presence *now*. In every moment of complete participation we awaken the real emptiness which is total fullness.

In the completeness of His oneness, everything has a part to play. In the wholeness of life, everything is included in a pattern of interdependent communion. Through participation we give ourselves to this wholeness. The drive for emptiness, for renunciation and self-denial, that has fueled our spiritual systems in the last centuries has only too easily been used to kill the fullness of life, to emphasize rejection and exclusion. The drive for transcendence has denied God's presence here. As we turn to life, as we involve ourselves completely in His world, we live the mystical union that sings in the essence of every atom of creation and strings together every element of the created world.

We can no longer lose ourselves by forgetting or denying ourselves. The emptiness at the core of our being is a vital emptiness that awakens as we give ourselves to life. When we are fully engaged in life there is an empty space where only our Beloved is present. And this presence is also all around us, in our ordinary lives, in the simplicity and complexity of ourself. In order to awaken to this divine presence, we must accept all of what life brings us and also accept the aspects of ourselves we have tried to reject and leave behind. Purification and transformation are no longer personal, but part of a larger unfolding. They allow us to give ourself to life and to our Beloved more fully, more completely. Giving ourself totally to life, we give ourself to our Beloved in a new way. Turning to life, we enter the stream of living oneness that runs through our hearts and the heart of the world in an unfathomable current of fullness. In this fullness where are we? Where is God?

We have forgotten that in oneness God's need is also our need. If He needs us to participate, if He needs us to embrace His world, then it is our own deepest need as well. For who are we to remain separate from Him? In our separation we are full of ourself and empty of Him; in oneness we are filled by Him and empty of ourselves. And yet as we live the oneness and multiplicity of our Beloved, all of ourself is included. Our desire for life is His desire to experience the wonder of His world. In oneness how can it be otherwise?

GIVING ONESELF TO LIFE

To participate in life as a whole means to give yourself to life as it is present around you, to respond to the need of the moment, to be open to what is offered wherever you are. We must not turn away from life; we must not deny what life brings us. We do not seek to change life, but to allow life to change itself through us. Through living our everyday life aligned with God, we give ourself to His work of transformation, to the uncovering of Himself in His world. All that holds us back is our concern for ourself, for our own material or spiritual well-being. Life takes us where we are needed and opens the door to our participation. All that is required of us is total participation.

Of course we will resist; our patterns of conditioning, particularly our spiritual conditioning, will hold us back. Spiritual conditioning has often told us to be separate from everyday life, to hide what is most precious from the crowds, from life around us. This may have been appropriate at one time, when the inner life of the spirit was emphasized and everyday life carried the shadow of spiritual aspiration. But those times have passed. We can no longer afford to split ourselves in pieces, to darken our daily life with disdain or disgust and offer our hearts only to a pure and transcendent light. Our love for God, our deepest and most sacred needs, must all be offered in every moment, to every detail of life. We are here to help the world come alive with divine love, to awaken humanity to a new level of consciousness. And this work cannot be done with an attitude of isolation, especially spiritual isolation. An attitude of isolation will separate us from the whole and we will not have access to the place on the inner planes where the work needs to be done.

Living in the midst of life, participating in the ordinary activities of the day, we align ourself with the inner plane of transformation that is being activated at this time. This plane of transformation can only be accessed from the midst of life, because that is where it is functioning. If we separate ourself from life we remain outside of the sphere of transformation.

But to give oneself to life does not in any way suggest limiting one's spiritual focus, one's inner alignment with God. What is needed is to bring these two together. Luckily this has always been the Sufi ideal, "outwardly to be with the people, inwardly to be with God." What is needed is a full acknowledgment of our own divinity and our own ordinariness. Holding those two seeming opposites allows us to participate in life from the highest level accessible to us as souls. It enables us to infuse our spiritual essence into the core of life, where it is most needed. It allows us to give ourself back to God in the midst of His world, and thus make the world once again alive with His presence.

Life needs us; life is calling to us, crying out to us. Life is opening doors that until now have been locked. And all that is required of us is to say, "Yes! I am here for Thy sake. Do with me as Thou will." This completeness of giving attracts the grace and power that are needed. It also attracts to us the situations in life where our participation is most effective. Most people forget that life is alive and gives us what we need.

We have become so identified with our own struggle that we think we have to find our way and make things happen. That may be so for those who are only concerned with the welfare of their own self, but if you are here in service to life, life responds. Life works together with you, teaching you, leading you, giving you every help and incentive. The more you give yourself to life, the more life responds. And if you give yourself to life for His sake, for the purpose of His work, then magic comes into your life and manipulates the patterns of reality to enable you to work more freely, to give yourself more completely.

Life is an expression of divine oneness and for the Sufi contains the mystery of the word *Kun!* (Be). We are an integral part of life's unfolding mystery, its wonder and glory. And we have the capacity to be conscious of life's oneness, just as we can recognize how every cell of creation carries an imprint of His name.

If we become conscious of life's oneness, then we respect our own divinity, because there is nothing other than God. Everything is He!—*Hama ust!*—and we have the capacity to know and live this oneness. This world is a place of His revelation of Himself to Himself, and we are a central part of this drama, this unfolding of love and knowledge. Our responsibility is to embrace this role, to be part of life, to love Him in His world. Hafiz explains this mystery:

> Stay close to those sounds
>
> The sun turns a key in a lock each day
> As soon as it crawls out of bed.
>
> Light swings open a door
> And the many kinds of love rush out
> Onto the infinite green field.
>
> Your soul sometimes plays a note
> Against the Sky's ear that excites
> The birds and planets.
>
> Stay close to any sounds
> That make you glad you are alive.
>
> Everything in this world is
> Helplessly reeling.

An invisible wake was created
When God said to His beautiful dead lover,
"Be."

Hafiz, who will understand you
If you do not explain that last line?
Well then,

I will sing it this way,

When God said to Illusion,
"Be."[2]

LIVING THE FREEDOM OF LOVE

God needs us to bring alive the mystery He has hidden
in His world. We are the agents of His self-revelation;
we hold the secrets of creation within our own hearts.
He needs us to know His oneness and to live this knowledge. And this knowledge carries with it the love that
belongs to oneness, because oneness is the consciousness of love. In love there is only oneness: the rose and
the thorn are one. The pain of separation belongs only
to the desire for union.

To become conscious of love is to be drawn into the
circle of oneness. Love always draws us back to oneness.
Even in a human love-affair we long to get closer and
closer to the one we love, to merge, to unite in the ec-
stasy of love-making that takes us beyond our separate
self. Love carries the knowledge of oneness. And those
who know the mysteries of love know how oneness
works in the world. They can see the patterns of oneness
that are unfolding, the wonder of *light upon light*, and
watch how that which had been hidden is revealed.

Real love is not to be confused with a desire for security or emotional bonding. Real love is a love that opens itself to all possibilities and is not caught in the patterns of limitation. It carries the song of freedom, just as it carries the imprint of Him who is freedom itself. It flows through all of life, and those who have given themselves to love, who have been taken by love, know how love comes into the world. They know the secret places where love manifests and is most accessible. And they need to give this knowledge to humanity.

In our culture we identify love mainly as belonging to human relationships. We even confuse it with passion, sexuality, or emotional need. And because our culture is dominated by the buying and selling of the marketplace, we project those same values onto love. We do not recognize that love is given freely, that its very nature is free. A child may think that she is loved because she behaves well, or does well in school, but this cannot be love. Nor can a partner be loved for any "reason," because this would limit love, contain it within the prison of cause and effect. Love cannot be bought or sold, or even traded. Love is like the sunlight, always present even above the clouds of our psychological blocks, our emotional problems, our patterns of self-denial.

But this love that belongs to us, that is the very substance of our being, needs to be lived with the freedom that is its nature. It needs to be brought into the marketplace of the world that has been polluted with thought-forms of greed and patterns of buying and selling.

When the currents of love flow with the joy that is the essence of life, there will be a healing beyond anything we could imagine. When the freedom of love infuses a world that knows mostly bargain and loss, craving and hoarding, then a strange and new alchemy can take place, and we can all watch the wild magic unfold.

REAL COOPERATIVE WORK

It is time to celebrate our real nature, our divinity, the oneness of life. It is time to remember the song of creation and how we are here to serve the Creator. We have lost touch with the simplicity of service, which Mother Teresa expresses so beautifully:

> It is not what you do, but the love that you put in the doing, because then you give it to God and He makes it infinite.
>
> It is not how much you give, but the love that you put in the giving, because then you give it to God and He makes it infinite.

We need to recognize that there is only one Giver, there is only one Healer. We need to work together with Him, not in the isolated castles of our own self-importance. Rûmî tells the moving story of the dervish who lived alone in the mountains. One day, while out picking fruit, he was mistakenly seized by the authorities who were looking for thieves nearby. The hermit's hand was cut off before his captors realized their mistake:

> He became known as Sheik Aqta.
> which means, "The teacher
> whose hand has been cut off."
>
> One day a visitor entered his hut without
>   knocking
> and saw him weaving palm leaf baskets.
> It takes two hands to weave!
>
> "Why have you entered without warning?"

"Out of love for you."

"Then keep this secret which you see
has been given to me."

But others began to know about this,
and many came to the hut to watch.

The hand that helped
when he was weaving palm leaves
came because he no longer had any fear
of dismemberment or death.

When those anxious, self-protecting
imaginations leave, the real,
cooperative work begins.[3]

One of our hands has been cut off by the vigilantes
of our collective beliefs, by those whose values have sto-
len the joy and magic from the world. Our Western culture has left the cupboard empty, the world desecrated.
Each morning we can see the handicap that has been
forced upon us. But we haven't yet learned to see our
affliction as an opportunity. We haven't learned to make
use of our helplessness, to allow our helplessness to call
down the grace that is available. We can learn the "real
cooperative work" of weaving with the invisible hand
that is always being offered. At this time of global need,
we must allow His mercy to return to life the sanctity for
which we all hunger.

Our Beloved is like a guest waiting to be invited, a
lover longing to be called. "I respond to the call of the
caller when he calls to Me." As the guardians of the
world, the intermediaries between heaven and earth, we
need to ask Him for His help to redeem His world. He

only asks that we put aside the burden of our woundedness, our armor of self-protection, and look beyond ourself to what He waits to give us.

BEYOND THE PHYSICAL PLANE

The physical world, composed of separate material objects, constantly separates us: we are separate from each other, from different geographic areas, and seemingly from the divine. This is part of the mystery of the physical plane, how it defines things by their separate nature. From the moment we get out of bed in the morning, each object is distinct: the toothbrush is separate from the toothpaste, the plate separate from the bread. In this world we are always aware of boundaries: the walls around us, the ground under our feet. This consciousness has permeated our human relationships, in which we automatically think of ourself as separate, only too aware of the boundaries of custom and the patterns of behavior that distance us from each other.

The mystic who has passed beyond the borders of physical consciousness knows that there is a different way to live, knows that the world as it appears is a mirage. Yes, the physical, tangible world is around us, but so are other levels of reality which are accessible to humanity. Nothing is fixed, separate, or static, and the laws that govern our existence are very different from the patterns of causality we pretend are the basis of life. Awakening to this deeper reality, the mystic sees the limitations we impose upon ourself, how we imprison ourself in a vision of life that is only one spectrum of consciousness.

Until now the mystic has mainly kept her experience a secret, shared only with members of her spiritual community. The mystic knows how in Plato's story of the cave, the man who frees himself from the chains and goes out into the sunlight is rejected as a madman when he returns to tell others that they are only seeing illusions, chasing shadows. So mystics have worked behind the scenes of life, using the understanding gained from their experiences to help humanity in hidden ways.

But the mystic is now needed to help free humanity from the limited spectrum of consciousness that imprisons us on the physical plane. The knowledge that mystics have kept secret needs to be made available. In particular, humanity needs to know the secrets of oneness, the plane of unity where all of life is perceived as an interrelated whole. Humanity needs this knowledge in order to take the next step in its evolution.

The plane of unity and the energy of this plane are being made accessible to humanity, but at present people do not recognize what is available. They do not know the possibilities of freedom and interdependent cooperation that are now being offered. If the plane of unity is seen only through the veils of physical consciousness, it does not reveal its magic and potential. Instead it becomes just another possibility for material progress. And because the patterns of physical consciousness create images of separation and division, this new energy potential will dramatically increase the experience of alienation. For example, computers can help us be more connected or they can leave us feeling more isolated, caught in a technological world that denies us ordinary, human contact.

The energy that belongs to the plane of unity is changing our awareness without our knowing. Daily we see news from around the world; we can communicate instantaneously anywhere. But we do not understand the greater implication that a whole new plane of awareness is being given to us. We see this development as just a further evolution of physical science and its child, technology. Thus we are missing the real potential of these changes. If we can access a different level of consciousness, we will see how these changes have far vaster implications. They are not just the next step but a totally different step.

The danger is that if we do not grasp the significance of these changes and, instead, use the knowledge and energy that are being made available solely for physical, material progress, the energy will become dangerously unbalanced. Christ, also speaking at a time of transition when a new energy and wisdom were being made available, said:

> Neither do men put new wine into old bottles: else the bottles break, and the wine runeth out, and the bottles perish: but they put new wine into new bottles, and both are preserved.[4]

The importance of embracing a new perspective of life cannot be overstressed. It not only brings possibilities; it is vital to our survival. The mystic has long known the oneness of all of creation, and how this physical oneness is just a part of a greater oneness. The mystic also knows that human beings have the potential to transcend the limitations of a consciousness constricted to the physical plane, to experience and work with the plane of unity that is always present. Knowing how this awareness will change our perception and experience of life and reconnect us to our essential wholeness, the mystic has a central role to play in the present time of transition. Mystics can help prepare humanity for the possibilities of the future in a very practical way. They can give their knowledge back to humanity so that we can all learn to work with the energy that is being made accessible. This knowledge can help us create the organic structures that will contain the "new wine," a wine that will nourish and intoxicate us with wonder and beauty, that will awaken us to the glory of divine presence.

The Plane of Unity

And in everything there is a witness for Him
that points to the fact that He is one.

Anonymous

RECOGNIZING THE EXISTENCE OF ONENESS

The first step is to recognize the plane of unity and know that we can attune ourself to it. Many people have had experiences of this primal unity, whether in meditation, in the silence of nature, at night looking into the star-filled heavens, or listening to a piece of music. For an instant we are transported beyond ourself into a vaster and simpler oneness. Full of awe and wonder we return to our everyday self, knowing that we have experienced something real yet undefined. These moments color our existence more than we realize, sometimes awakening us to a new quality of life, sometimes haunting us with a sense of lost paradise.

Poets and mystics have written of these states. William Blake describes the simple beauty of his vision:

> To see a World in a Grain of Sand
> And a Heaven in a Wild Flower.
> Hold Infinity in the palm of your hand
> And Eternity in an hour.[1]

The thirteenth-century Sufi Farîduddîn 'Attâr, who has seen God's presence in every atom and knows that "in Your Presence there cannot be two," points us directly towards unity:

> Invoke the One, desire the One, search the One
> See the One—know the One and affirm that it is
>   One
> Whether at the beginning or at the end, all of this
>   is only one single thing
> Alas the eye of man sees double.[2]

Although we see with the eyes of duality, the vision of unity is waiting for us. We can all awaken to this plane of consciousness, experience moments in which oneness is revealed to us. Many people who have had experiences of this dimension do not recognize their value or meaning. Overawed for an instant, they return to their ordinary consciousness in which such experiences seem out of place. And so this glimpse into the underlying fabric of reality becomes just a memory. Pushed aside by the demands of life, it stays hidden within us, a secret even from our own knowing.

But if we recognize the significance of such experiences, we can integrate them into ordinary perception, and they can become the foundation for a different quality of awareness. Knowing the oneness that is inherent in all of life can revolutionize our relationship to life and to ourselves. In oneness our real place in the wholeness of life is made known, and this gives us a sense of belonging and the true individuality that comes from this real belonging. Gradually the meaning of oneness will grow within us, giving birth to the child of the future—a way to live in harmony with ourself and all of life.

Children often live unconsciously in this world, before the patterns of conditioning cut them off from their natural self. Many children also live with a closeness to God that is denied their parents. Accepting the world of adults, children sadly put aside this natural communion and close their eyes to the wonder of the world.

The awareness of unity is being given to humanity and it can awaken us to our own natural wholeness, our communion with life and with the divine. Wholeness includes the divine: in the oneness He is present. What is present within all of life, within every atom of creation, will be returned to us. The natural joy of life will again be present, not just in rare instances, but as something normal. And in this joy the divine is also present, because joy is an expression of the wonder of being alive, in which every atom sings His presence.

We need to learn again to see with the eyes of wholeness. This is what is being offered to humanity. It is already present but unnoticed. We are so conditioned to work and struggle that we do not appreciate what is being freely given. Looking only to the physical, we do not see the signs of His invisible help, His intangible presence.

THE DANCE OF REVELATION

We have been living in a world in which He appears to be absent. The notion that we have been banished from paradise, from the presence of God, is fundamental to our mythologies. This world has become a place of exile that is no longer sacred. We carry the scars of our banishment and our abandonment more than we realize. But who has been banished? What has really been abandoned?

Reclaiming the wholeness of the world, we will find that He is no longer absent. The veils that separated us from His living presence will be lifted, because wholeness makes visible the stamp of the divine. What had been hidden will be revealed. The mystery of His self-revelation will continue as He makes Himself known to Himself more fully.

The mystical secret that "wheresoever you turn, there is the Face of God" does not have to remain known by only a few. As unity awakens us to a very different relationship with life, we will be able to participate in the wonder of His awakening presence. The divine comes alive again not just within our hearts but within the whole of our life:

> How wonderful that a single Essence should
> Refract itself like light, a single source
> Into a million essences and hues.[3]

Until now this mystery has been known to only a few. Only a few have been allowed to consciously participate in the dynamic of revelation, watching the flow of energy as it comes into manifestation, bringing with it the fragrance, the qualities of His hidden nature. Mystics have watched as the ever-changing dynamic of life manifests the unchangeable essence, how out of the depths of silence, sounds awaken, how the myriad forms of life pour from the emptiness. Mystics have seen the interplay of the inner and outer, of what is hidden and what is revealed, and even laughed at the paradoxical nature of this process:

> if creatures were made to *reveal* Him, why are they
> veiled?
> But then, of course, veils themselves are very
> revealing...[4]

The mystic who makes the journey back to the source uncovers this wonder: how the one divine Being becomes so many and yet still remains one. But this quality of knowing is no longer being restricted to the few. The evolution of humanity moves forward, His revelation becoming always more complete. All those who turn towards God will be able to consciously participate in His revelation: how the one and the many reflect each other.

We consider the future within the framework of conditioned consciousness with its patterns of linear progression. But the dance of revelation does not follow any logical patterns. The Beloved comes to meet us again and again: He recognizes us even if we do not recognize Him. A linear future will give us the advances of technology, while the possibility of revelation allows Him to work miracles: to change the patterns of our knowing and awaken us to a future that is not born from the past but from the eternal now.

CONSCIOUS PARTICIPATION

Beyond the prison walls of our own knowing is a world so dynamic that the rules of our constriction do not apply. This is becoming apparent in the field of modern technology, which is changing our world faster than we understand. And this is only the beginning. What is being offered to humanity is access to a plane of consciousness that moves much faster than the physical world.

We have been thrown into this "brave new world" but only see it from a physical perspective. We see the fruits of technology with the eyes of the past, conditioned by materialism. We do not yet realize what we are being offered; we do not see that the technological revolution is just a physical manifestation of a whole new spectrum of consciousness. What is being given is beyond our present comprehension, and if we stay within our present attitudes we will never grasp its potential. We need to go beyond our fears and step into the vortex of this new energy, this dynamic oneness.

If we allow ourselves to be open, we will be shown the possibilities of oneness, the world beyond our prison walls. If we remain within the patterns of our present consciousness, isolated by our fears of what is new, then we will not be able to read the signs of revelation. We will be unable to consciously participate with the new energy, and it will never realize its potential. This new energy requires our *conscious participation*, because it is an energy of oneness, and its transformative potential can only be activated if we play our part in the whole.

The energy of oneness is waiting for us to align ourselves with it. Then it can speak to us and show us the way to work with it. It can come into our life and transform us with the qualities of oneness. An awareness of our interrelationship with the whole of life is only part of its potential. This energy has many different functions, has the possibility to change life in many different ways. It can work on many different levels, from the spiritual dimension of realizing our oneness with God, to the material plane where the physical resources of the planet will find their way to all those in need.

The energy of oneness will enable His oneness to become manifest and all of life to participate in the joy of His presence. It will give us access to knowledge based upon oneness, including a new understanding of healing, as well as technologies that are now in their infancy. All this wisdom is waiting for our participation. But we must step beyond our ego-centered identities to access it. This is why the first steps of recognizing the existence of the plane of unity and accepting that we can attune ourself with it are so important. Without making these steps we will remain within the shadowlands of our ego-oriented material culture, not noticing the dawn as it breaks around us.

THE WORK OF THE MYSTIC

The wisdom of oneness is waiting to be discovered and brought into consciousness. Our work is to enable this to happen, to stand on the borders of this new age and welcome the changes that are taking place. It is important to realize that these changes are happening primarily in the inner world at present, and it is here that the mystic is needed.

The mystic is familiar with a reality not delineated by physical form, a reality that belongs to the inner world of meditation and prayer. In our aspiration we look beyond the world of appearances to what is hidden within us. We come to know a presence that permeates our outer life and yet is not caught in its constriction. We feel the freedom, intimacy, and awe that belong to this "other." We have found a fragrance not of this world, tasted a love that nourishes us, heard a silence that beckons to us. We have awakened to a different quality of knowing, one that comes to us in dreams, intuitions, hints, or visions.

The plane of unity has always been accessible to the mystic. It is the locus of the soul's journey. The soul calls us back to our inborn state of oneness. At the beginning of our journey we are given just a glimpse of this natural oneness, a sip of the wine that belongs to love's unity. Later, after we have walked through the desert of separation, we are given a deepening sense of our real belonging. In moments of meditation, the heart opens to the oneness that underlies everything, and in waking consciousness we become attuned to the signs of His oneness, the way He reveals His presence.

For the lover, the plane of unity is experienced through love. We long for our Beloved and His love draws us to Him, freeing us of the chains of separation, the illusion of duality. Going deep within the heart, we find that He is always with us, until His love drowns us in the vast ocean of oneness.

The practices of the path draw us into this inner world, and we become familiar with its ways. We recognize a knowing in which there is not the division of knower and knowledge, a love that does not carry the chains of duality. We sense a quality of being that just *is*. The energy of the path attunes us to the frequency of oneness, and helps us live this inner alignment in the outer world. As "soldiers of the two worlds," we hold His oneness within the heart as we interact with the multiplicity of life. Now we need to consciously recognize what we have been given, where we have been taken, so that we can participate more fully in the work of aligning the world with oneness.

How do we do a work that until now has been veiled in secrecy, when so much of its knowledge has only been hinted at? The simplicity of oneness is that we are always given everything we need. Working with oneness is to work with completeness: everything is present at each moment in time. But we need to make a shift from an attitude that sees what is missing, what is absent, to an awareness of wholeness. If we look with the eye of wholeness we will see the work that needs to be done, that is calling for our attention. It is a simple reorientation of consciousness.

However, one of the difficulties is that we have to orient ourself towards a reality that is not yet manifest, that exists on the inner plane rather than in the outer world of forms. It is on the inner plane that the energy structure of oneness is being made accessible to us, and it is here that our participation is required. This is a participation of awareness rather than "doing," reflecting the Taoist attitude of "work without doing." Our conscious participation as a state of awareness is needed. If we consciously connect with the energy that is being made accessible, this energy will flow where it is needed through our awareness. It will come down into the plane of manifestation as a creative rather than destructive force.

The consciousness of the mystic is needed to channel the energy of love and oneness into the world. Until now the mystic has done this work primarily unconsciously, unknowingly, veiled even from herself. The hiddenness was needed to protect the individual from the corruptive possibilities of such knowledge. It is only too easy for the ego to become inflated or get caught in power dynamics. But now the energy of oneness will not manifest in its full potential without consciousness. We need to know that we are working to bring this energy into the world, even if this knowledge challenges us with the dangers of inflation.

What has been hidden is being revealed, and we are needed to consciously participate in this process of revelation. Our consciousness is being used to make His oneness known to the world.

THE DEVELOPMENT OF CONSCIOUSNESS

Until now the development of consciousness has made us aware of our individual self as different from others. This is the drama most people begin to experience in adolescence as they fight to claim their individuality,

their separate sense of self. Sadly, this journey of indi-
viduation often brings with it a feeling of isolation that
easily becomes anger or despair. As we claim something
for ourself, there is also a sense of something that is being
denied or taken away.

We become aware of our individual nature by recognizing how we are different from our parents, family, or
friends. Consciousness takes us on a journey of separation that has a very powerful effect in all aspects of life.
We are not even aware of how much we experience life
through this paradigm of separation. Nor do we realize
that the next step in consciousness is to regain our sense
of unity. This is not the undifferentiated oneness of un-
consciousness, the instinctual world in which there is no
growth or development. Rather, it is the oneness that
reveals our individuality within the whole and shows
how our unique note belongs to the symphony of life.
Through the whole we come to realize our purpose and
sense of self more fully.

Until now only those seekers who had stepped away
from the collective and traveled their own solitary path
have had access to the consciousness of unity. The door
to this quality of consciousness was only opened to individuals who had passed certain trials, who had faced the
darkness of their shadow and purified their lower nature.[5] The wonder of the present transition is that the
collective is being given access to this next step in consciousness without having to make this laborious and
painful inner journey. Now the doorway to unity stands
open to the whole of humanity.

The work of the mystic is to make human beings
aware of this possibility, to stand within the doorway of
unity and welcome the collective inside. Most people
do not even know that a consciousness beyond self-
oriented individuality exists. They do not see the light

that is streaming through, the wholeness that is beckoning them. The patterns of our collective conditioning have created a veil which blocks our awareness of what is being given. If we do not know what is being offered, we will not be able to fully participate in its magic, in its new way of being. We will not step through the doorway.

Even many spiritual seekers still think in terms of effort, of trials and tests. But there is no longer any key needed to open this door. It cannot now be closed.

This change is so simple and fundamental it is easy to overlook. It is not a problem to be solved. There is nothing to be learned, no steps to success. Something is being given freely, with no strings attached. All that is required is for each of us to say "yes."

The Heart of the World

In that abyss I saw how love held bound
Into one volume all the leaves whose flight
Is scattered through the universe around.

Dante[1]

THE SONG OF THE HEART OF THE WORLD

"I am He whom I love, He whom I love is me" is stamped within the heart of the lover. This oneness of love that is awakened within us activates the currents of love that gradually dissolve us, until we come to know the reality of oneness in both the inner and outer world. Mystics learn to live His oneness, first as a secret within the heart, and then as a knowledge that infuses itself through our whole being. The oneness within the heart awakens us to the oneness throughout all of life, and reveals how we remain unique within this oneness. In the words of Ibn ʿArabî:

> When the mystery—of realizing that the mys-
> tic is one with the Divine—is revealed to you, you
> will understand that you are no other than God
> and that you have continued and will continue...
> without when and without times. Then you will
> see all your actions to be His actions and all your
> attributes to be His attributes and your essence to
> be His essence, though you do not thereby become
> He or He you, in either the greatest or the least
> degree. "Everything is perishing save His Face,"
> that is, there is nothing except His Face, "then,
> whithersoever you turn, there is the Face of God."[2]

His love continually reminds us of His oneness, and it helps us to live it. The practice of the mystic is to stay in remembrance, to stay attuned to the energy of love that gives us the knowledge of the ways of oneness. Humanity needs to know how oneness works in the world, how His love reveals His Face and how in this revelation we can come to know our true nature.

But how can this knowledge be given to humanity when humanity has forgotten Him, when the gates of remembrance appear to be closed? How can we become attuned to oneness if we do not have any awareness of His presence? For the mystic, knowledge is infused into the heart, which is the organ of higher consciousness. Can this be given to the whole of humanity? Can the heart of the world be awakened to the higher knowledge of oneness?

What is happening within the world is an act of grace, as He reveals Himself to Himself in a new way. The knowledge that is needed to help in this time of transition is being given, but we have to be receptive to it—to know that it is here. This requires us to take a step away from our insular attitudes and become attuned, not just to our own heart, but also the heart of the world. Something is awakening within the heart of the world that needs our attention.

The heart of the world is beginning to sing the song of divine remembrance, but no one is listening; no one is attentive. We have even forgotten that the world has a heart. Medieval texts image man as a microcosm of the world, but we dismissed this symbolic relationship, just as we rejected the older vision of the earth as a living being. As the world stopped being a sacred or symbolic reality and became just matter governed by the laws of physics, so the heart, or "soul of the world" (*anima mundi*), was discarded as a myth.

But now the heart of the world is beginning to sing. No one even knows that the heart of the world can sing. It has been so long, so many ages have passed, since this last happened. It is not in the annals of our recorded history. But if it goes unnoticed a moment of great opportunity will have passed, and in the depths of humanity, in the soul of the world, there will remain a deep sadness of regret.

Only if we step aside from our own pursuits, material or spiritual, can we hear the heart of the world. If we are busy with our own worldly success or spiritual redemption we will be too self-absorbed to notice.

But if enough people hear the heart of the world awakening, hear the song of joy and love that is waiting to be sung, then we will all be able to participate in this happening. In the heart of the world is the knowledge of the world's own healing and transformation. In the heart of the world are the love and power that are needed for this work. And we contain the heart of the world within our own hearts. This is one of mankind's secrets, hidden from us until now.

"Man is My secret and I am his secret." We are made in the image of God and are also the microcosm of His creation. Our own heart is directly linked to the heart of the world, just as it is directly linked to His unknowable essence.[3] We contain the secrets of the universe within our own heart. At different times, in different eras, we are given access to different secrets, different ways of knowing and different qualities of knowledge. This is the way "evolution" functions.

The heart of the world needs to know that we have heard it, that we are attentive to its awakening. Then it will tell us what we need to know. This knowing is being given directly to the hearts and minds of those who are listening, who are attentive. It is given to each of us according to our own nature and the work that we need to do. It is totally individual, because this is the way oneness works in the world.

The knowledge that is being given also contains the energy needed to do this work. The power and love that are present within the heart of the world can awaken us to the feeling of joy that our life is lacking, and the freedom that belongs to this joy. Those who know how divine love works will recognize this energy, because they have experienced it in their own life. They know the simplicity of what is given, and how this love returns us to our own essential nature.

The love and knowledge in the heart of the world cannot be traded. If we try to use it for personal ends it will become distorted and lose its magic. There will be no joy. But if we live it for His sake, then it will grow and flourish and reveal its real potential. Then, in the first time for many generations, we will come to know why we are here. Our personal and collective destiny will come into harmony, and the song in our own heart and the song of the heart of the world will resonate together. For some people this is already happening, and it is like the sun breaking through after a long winter, like the colors of spring flowers showing themselves through the grayness of our polluted world.

AN ORGANIC WEB OF ENERGY

We can access the heart of the world through our own heart, and in particular through the dynamic presence of a spiritual group. At different times the energy structure of the world is accessed in different ways. For many ages sacred buildings with their geometric designs enabled the higher inner energy of the planet to be used for the benefit of the people. In the present time the most powerful vehicles of transformation are spiritual groups, which are being given direct access to high levels of energy.

Spiritual groups are forming and being placed all across the planet where the energy of transformation is needed. They are creating an organic web, a membrane of light and love, that will soon be activated globally. Until now many groups have not been aware that they are a part of this dynamic organism, but have been working individually according to their own spiritual traditions. But as the energy begins to flow throughout this web, each group will come alive in a new way, responding to the need of the time.

This web of light and love will be the container for the energy of the new age, an energy of love and oneness, and it will be formed within the hearts of those who are attuned to this work. The heart is a very powerful center of spiritual consciousness, as expressed in the *hadith*, "Heaven and earth contain Me not, but the heart of My devoted servant contains Me." The heart of an awakened human being contains the divine consciousness of the soul, our conscious connection to the divine oneness.

This organic web of love and devotion is gradually forming. Small parts of it are already being activated, being brought together on the inner planes where the connections are being made. When the energy begins to flow between these groups, a dynamic shift will take place. The analogy to the Internet through which information flows through certain "hubs" is not coincidental. The energy structure of the planet is being set up similarly on different levels. This has to do with the optimum way energy can flow in the next age. This organic structure is composed of individual groups that function totally independently, just as individual personal computers in a network function independently. This structure of linked groups will be able to work with the energy of the new age, an energy that gives each individual the potential to live her unique nature. Once the energy flowing through this organic web reaches a certain point, then the organic structure wakes up and functions as a dynamic living entity. This is when the possibilities of the new age will become a living reality. This is when the higher consciousness of the planet will become activated.

This has not yet happened. Certain "tests" are taking place to see how the structure could work. Different groups, different spiritual traditions, are coming together first on the inner planes and then outwardly, to see the effects and the reactions to this dynamic. An organic web of interrelated entities will challenge the present hierarchical power structures. But because the web has no "central core" to attack, hierarchical power structures will not know how to respond.[4]

An organic structure is more fluid and dynamic than any hierarchical organization. And there comes a moment when the energy flow around the web responds of its own accord to the need of the moment. The energy then just flows in a different way, making new connections as required so that it can get to where it is needed. And the individuals who are part of this structure respond in synchronism, as happens in any living organism. This is an optimum system for bringing energy, knowledge, or physical resources to where they are needed. It utilizes human beings' capacity to work together as part of a unified field of consciousness, without imposing any structure or conditions. This is part of the potential of the consciousness of oneness that is being given to humanity, that is being awakened within the heart of the world.

A NEW SPECTRUM OF CONSCIOUSNESS

The potency, power, and transformational potential of the energy that is being awakened will depend upon how we live it. If we use it for our own personal benefit, it will fracture, causing chaos. If we use it for the purpose of the whole, it will flourish and flow more freely. This energy is directly attuned to our own conscious participation, which makes it more dynamic and also more dangerous. It requires a greater degree of responsibility than we have been accustomed to. It also has the potential to awaken spiritual centers within human beings, some of which have never before been activated. This awakening can happen both within the collective body of humanity and within individuals.

The activation of spiritual centers gives us access to a different spectrum of consciousness. For example, there is a spectrum of consciousness in which the possibilities for the future are visible. The future is not defined. Rather, it is a fluid, organic pattern that can evolve in different ways. The ancient Chinese text, *I Ching*, or *Book of Changes*, written according to the principles of this spectrum of consciousness, describes how the attitude of the individual and the events that occur work together. The hexagrams of the *I Ching* describe life's flow of energy in poetic images. If one has access to this spectrum of consciousness, one can creatively work with the energy of life as it determines the future, rather than always responding to events that have already happened.

Once an event has already happened on the physical plane, the energy of life has crystallized into a form, and it is much more difficult to influence or resolve. When we interact with events after they have crystallized, we become involved in patterns of action and reaction, or "conflict resolution." Working with the energy flow of life rather than with events that have already taken place will allow us to have a more dynamic and creative relationship with life. We will be able to see where energy patterns could form into dangerous bottlenecks, where too much energy is concentrated at a particular point. With this knowledge we can take precautions to stop a catastrophe, or even divert a flow of energy before trouble starts.

There is also the potential to work with the possibilities inherent in a situation before it comes into form so that it can realize its greatest benefit, its most creative outcome. Working with the energy patterns of life and the spectrum of consciousness that sees how they can affect the future gives humanity the potential to live in a very different way. These energy patterns will also reveal how interdependent we are, how much our attitudes and actions affect each other. It will help us to dissolve our insular approach and to work together.

THE LINK OF LOVE

The heart of the world is waiting for human beings to access its wisdom and love, waiting for us to participate in this opening. Because the energy of transformation has not yet reached the physical plane, there is nothing to "do" in outer terms; rather this participation is an attitude of receptivity, of awareness, of attention. Participating in this way, we become attuned to a connection that is being made within the consciousness of the heart. Through this link of love that connects us to the heart of the world, we will have access to the knowledge and energy that are being given. This connection will be clearer, stronger, more accessible, depending upon our nature. Some will only sense its presence through the veil of their desires and conditioning, while others have been waiting the whole of their lives for this connection and feel the joy that it brings. But we each have our part to play in the unfolding of love.

Walking through the shadowlands of our culture, we see the debris of consumerism, whether material, mental, or spiritual. Our hearts have always cried for the truth of something other, of a way of being that is not bound by the gravitational pull of the ego. We have sensed what has been waiting for us for so long. And yet when the moment arrives we can hardly believe it.

Those who have followed their own individual dreams know the reality of inner transformation. They have touched, however briefly, the infinite dimension of their own self. And yet we have been conditioned to believe that is only a solitary venture, accessible to the few. Why should we limit the grace of God and the possibilities for humanity?

Mystics, lovers, spiritual wayfarers are those who follow the signs in the unseen world, who walk a path that others say is just a dream. But we know the reality of this dream, and have given our life to follow it. We know that real changes happen first inwardly before they manifest in outer life. And we know that we have to free ourself from any pattern of thinking, from any imposed attitude, in order to embrace the vaster truth of our real nature.

There are no road maps because the road has not yet been made. There is no certainty because nothing has come into the world of forms. Nothing is defined; it is only hinted at. And as in all times of transition, a sacrifice is necessary. We have to sacrifice our concern with our own progress, with our own inner journey. If we look too closely towards ourself, we will not see what is happening. We will remain isolated and unable to participate.

Those who are crazy enough to be mystics long to put aside any cloak of self-interest, to embark on a mad venture, guided only by their dreams and the stars. The heart of the world is calling to us and we are here to respond to the call of the heart. We are in tune with the currents of love that flow into the world. And more important, we are here for His sake. We belong to His oneness and not to ourselves. If our heart is called, we follow, drawn by the thread of His love for us, which is the thread of love that runs through humanity, the primal truth of "He loves them and they love Him."

If He needs us to put aside the focus on our own journey, we will gladly respond. If this means to sacrifice our longing for the beyond so that we can be here more fully, engage more completely, we will sacrifice even our aspiration for Him, our desire to dissolve completely in love. We are His servants, and the only desire of the servant is to serve his master.

If we lose everything in this adventure, what does it matter? What do we care for ourself? We know that we are a part of our Beloved, just a piece of dust in His garden. Again and again we give ourself to Him. Lifetime after lifetime we long to serve Him. Once again it is time to put aside the burdens of ourself and step into this fire of service, this joy of sacrifice. We have to sacrifice our suffering and our spirituality; even our aspiration needs to be placed on the altar of the heart. If we are to awaken the joy of His presence, everything has to go. And many of us have for years been bored with ourselves, even with our spiritual progress. We have sensed that there is something else we are here to do.

If we are crazy enough to sacrifice everything, then we will have direct access to the energy of love that is being given to awaken the world to unity. Our heart will be directly aligned to the heart of the world and the energy that is being given. Everything we need is present, but as always what stands in our way is our own self. The ecstatic mystic Bâyezîd Bistâmî, who was immersed in unity, expressed this primal truth:

> I saw my Lord in my dreams and I asked, "How am I to find You?" He replied, "Leave yourself and come!"

The sacrifice of our own self is repeated lifetime after lifetime. In each time He requires of us a new sacrifice, a new way to show our devotion. There were times when we had to sacrifice our attachment to the physical world, take up the staff of the ascetic; or our attachment to learning, when, like Rûmî, we met our Shams, and our books burned as we drowned in love. We have to prove our devotion again and again, sacrificing that which seems most precious. Only then does He take us into the inner mysteries of love where we are branded into service.

This time we have to sacrifice our own attachment to spiritual life, to anything that separates us from the whole. We have to give up the fruits of our aspiration and the spiritual conditioning we have acquired. We have to leave the space of spiritual protection and accept our responsibility to the whole, because we know in our heart that there is nothing other than He.

Spiritual Security

Do not worry about anything ever,
For the grace of God is in every shape and form.

Sufi Saying

REFUGE FROM THE WORLD

We all seek security on different levels. We look to money or property for physical security. We find emotional security from a partner, family, or friends. We use knowledge to provide mental security. And we can find spiritual security from spiritual life, from the sense of peace and inner well-being that we experience through meditation or other practices. During times of transition any state of security, whether material or spiritual, can become an obstacle, inhibiting our ability to move to a different dimension or quality of awareness.

The wayfarer knows the dangers of physical security, how easily we can become caught in patterns of accumulation. The material world draws us into its *maya* with the promise of protection, until we become a prisoner of our increasing need and desperation. Patterns of emotional security and their shadow dynamics of co-dependency are less visible but just as constraining.

The wayfarer knows these obstacles, these well-decorated prison walls. She knows that the material world does not offer anything lasting, and that the knowledge of the mind can be forgotten. Less obvious is how the patterns of spiritual security can become limiting, how even inner peace can become a prison. But anything that offers us refuge constellates the dangers of which we are afraid. Any desire to find protection creates a demon from which we must escape.

Spiritual security has many forms, some more subtle than others. There is the basic security offered by meditation or prayer, in which we are able to turn away from the world and rest in inner silence. However, this inner silence has conditions. It is a container of peace that shuts out the noise of the world, the physical and emotional dissonance of our lives. But it is not the dynamic, unstructured dimension of Reality.

Through our meditation and other practices we create a structure on the inner plane whose purpose is to protect us from energies that might interfere with our spiritual aspiration. We create a container of light and love that enables us to listen in silence, to see with clarity, to love without distortion. This is an important stepping stone on the path, to create an inner place where we can be in silence and tranquility, where we can listen to the voice of the Self and feel the depths that are hidden within us.

But if it is too strong, the container separates us too much from the world. If our spiritual practice evokes a need to retire that no longer nourishes us, no longer gives us the energy we need for our lives, then we have traded real spirituality for safety and security. As with a drug we become dependent on its tranquility, addicted to the peace it offers. Our meditation remains static, a place of refuge rather than a place of dynamic offering and unfolding.

Without knowing it, we stagnate, contracted by our ideals of spiritual life. We may become aloof, slightly untouched and unreachable. When too much energy is drawn inward, we can lose contact with the flow of life that requires our participation. Gradually everyday activities become draining and we want to do less and less. Only our spiritual practice seems to offer meaning. This is when the walls of protection become imprisoning, and our spiritual practice has become another pattern of escape.

Patterns of protection are very subtle. They form beneath the surface and create a web of conditioning that saps our energy without our knowing it. They gain a life of their own, and require constant maintenance. Our need for protection feeds our antagonism to the world, which in turn increases our need to retreat. This inescapable cycle cuts us off more and more from the fast-flowing river of life where the names of God are becoming visible, where the signs of our Beloved are waiting to be read.

The signs of God can only be read if we are fully present in life. The hidden substance of life only reveals its potential through our complete participation. Only then do its magic and meaning, its ways of revealing the divine, become activated. Life needs the presence of those who belong to God in order to become awake. If our spiritual practice isolates us from life, from the completeness of creation, then we miss the opportunity that is being offered.

The sacrifice that many wayfarers have to make now is the desire for security and safety. His protection is always present, and the more we give ourself to Him the more He is with us. But the way this protection is given changes according to "the time and the place and the people." Specifically it should not create a barrier between us and wholeness of life. He does not separate us from His world.

There have been times when this attitude of withdrawal was the path to reach Reality. The cloister or hermitage offered a refuge from a corruptive or dangerous world where spiritual life could not be practiced.

Working with Oneness

Inner contemplation opened the doors of revelation, and outer life was dismissed as an obstacle or *maya*.

But these times have passed. The world can no longer afford to have its spirituality denied. The world is living, and like all living things, needs care and nourishment, needs to be related to, needs the opportunity to offer itself within love. Mystics, knowing that "the world is no more than the Beloved's single face," bring into life the attention life needs and can turn towards the world and seek its hidden substance. In this time of great possibility, of infinite horizons, can we bear to limit God? Can we bear to limit ourselves?

TOUCHING THE DARKNESS

Through our desire for light we restrict the creativity of darkness; through our pursuit of purity we kill the alchemical magic of corruption. Spiritual practice has for so long drawn us towards our goals of perfection that we have lost the true freedom of hopelessness, the wild joy of disorientation, the erotic wonder of being spun into nowhere. Real spirituality demands that we take a step towards that which we reject. Not with the intention of integration or the ideal of wholeness, but with the utter simplicity that God needs us there.

What is it that we have been hiding, and hiding from? What is it that keeps us desperately looking straight ahead, avoiding the dark currents that can suddenly deter and command us? Uncharted territory is the only landscape worth exploring. When will we finally summon the courage to go where there are no maps and no warning signs?

For too long we have cut ourselves off from the potency of darkness, from the energy source hiding within

the obscured, the forgotten, the underground. The darkness is real and dangerous, but it carries a power and
energy that we need. Like chaos, darkness carries the
energy of creation, what is undefined, undifferentiated,
what is not yet limited by form. There is treasure in what
we have ignored. There is a stream of golden honey run-
ning through the veins of the earth, along the currents
at the bottom of the ocean. In the dark and forbidden
places, where the wind is wild and unsettling, we can
discover a passion and magic that belong to us. When
we touch these places for His sake, without concern
for ourselves, without intention to learn or grow, but
only to live more fully, to give ourself more completely,
something can finally happen, something can finally
be released.

Complete surrender to God allows us to touch the
darkness of the world for His sake. Surrender is the only
true protection for the servant, the only place of real
security. Without surrender, when we enter the darkness we will be taken by it, consumed and lost, of no
further use. Today, real spiritual protection does not hide
us from life, but invites us completely into life, into the
dark places that need our attention. The way we stay
protected in such darkness was imaged in a dream a
friend had just before returning to work on Wall Street
after a year away:

> There is a satanic presence or entity. And there
> is a small group, maybe four people. A man in the
> group has come to warn the others that the food is
> tainted. The platter of food looks fresh and deli-
> cious. But because of the man's warning, I know,
> without actually seeing it, that the food is actually
> vile and rotten, maggot-infested. That the food is

a kind of temptation, rotten in reality but wholesome and appetizing in appearance.

A woman in the group leaves the others, enters a yellow room and closes the door. Because of the energy she carries, the satanic presence cannot penetrate into the room. But I can see through the crack, where the door meets the wall, what is outside. It is like the energy of chaos, the energy of the universe before creation, before there was any form. Orange electrical charges crackling in every direction, incredibly dynamic and chaotic and wild.

The woman could stay in the yellow room and keep the satanic presence at bay. But instead she lets the energy she carries start flowing through her and out beyond the door. I can feel the energy beginning to flow. I remember no more of the dream.

In the encounter with the world of power and money, the satanic presence is very real. And the food offered by this world is tainted. It appears fresh and delicious, but this is just a temptation. The attractions of our culture may appear to be nourishing, but inwardly they are corruptive. The temptations of power, money, and material success eat away at our integrity. In the world of Wall Street the temptations are obvious, but any wayfarer who goes into the marketplace of the world will be offered similar temptations. This is a part of the archetypal drama of the soul, imaged in the temptations of Christ.

Today's wayfarer has to face the *maya* of the world directly, to consciously recognize the rottenness of what it appears to offer. The dreamer finds a place of protection, a yellow room, where the satanic energy cannot enter. This is the inner sanctum created by spiritual practice. Because the dreamer belongs to the Naqshbandi Sufi path, whose color is golden yellow, the color of this room is yellow. Our spiritual superiors and the energy of the path protect us.

In the dream the woman could stay within the yellow room, but then she would remain isolated. Instead she lets the energy she carries flow through her and beyond the door. This is the moment of transition. Inwardly she remains within the room and is protected; outwardly she begins to interact with life, reflecting one of the basic Sufi principles, "Outwardly to be with the people, inwardly to be with God."

And what is this "energy of chaos, the energy of the universe before creation, before there was any form," with its "orange electrical charges crackling in every direction, incredibly dynamic and chaotic and wild"? Unlike the corrupted food, the temptations of money and power, this is the primal energy of life that needs our participation. At the dawn of a new age, this is the new energy that has not yet come into manifestation. Dynamic and powerful, it has not yet constellated into any form. We are being asked to work with this energy, so that it can come into life resonating with the name of God. If we interact with this energy from the highest level, it can bring His remembrance into the whole of life.

As the energy of our devotion meets this unformed energy of chaos, new life can be born that does not belong to the patterns of separation but sings the song of divine unity. This is the potential of this moment. We have the possibility to align the energy of life with what is highest within humanity and be co-creators of our own world. Then the destiny of humanity will resonate with the joy of life that recognizes its divinity.

SPIRITUAL DISCRIMINATION

How can one walk the thin line between the need for spiritual protection and the necessity to fully participate in life? Without the awareness and guidance that come from our spiritual orientation, we cannot discriminate between the food of life that is nourishing and that which is rotten and poisonous. Our spiritual practices help free us from the grip of *maya* and enable us to see behind the façade of appearances. Once our desires no longer dominate us, once the light breaks through the curtains of our conditioning, we can see with the discrimination of the Self that recognizes that which corrupts and that which gives sustenance. Unfortunately there is no rule-book to follow, and each circumstance must be treated individually. Material desires are not always to be dismissed, and what appears spiritual can easily be a more subtle illusion, another power dynamic or pattern of co-dependency.

Attentive to every step, we walk the dusty roads of the world. We know that everything is He, and yet the world also contains forces of light and forces of darkness. We know that anger and hatred are real, and that the forces of materialism do not like what is given freely. If a whole culture depends upon the process of buying and selling, it has much to lose from what is free. The mystic knows a different dimension where love and energy flow without restriction, where all those in need are given to. This is why the mystic is always a threat to those who hold positions of power.

The mystic rarely seeks confrontation, knowing that it only focuses the forces of antagonism. It is usually easier to subvert the patterns of power than confront them. This is how the Beloved comes to us despite our defenses, "like a thief in the night." Somehow we always leave the back door unlocked, and this is also true of the collective. Everything longs for love, for the sunlight that is real nourishment. Even in the densest patterns of material desire there is a longing for something that cannot be named, cannot be grasped. We all hunger for what is Real.

Working with the oneness of life, we are held and contained by this oneness. We know that everything belongs to God, that His light is hidden even in the darkest corner. We learn to work with this hidden light, with humanity's deepest longing. The light of our own devotion guides us where we are needed, shows us the back door that is left open. Because we belong to our Beloved, we have nothing to lose. No one can take away the freedom of love, no one can deny us our servanthood.

And yet we have to be careful, to tread softly through the minefield that is the marketplace. We learn when to speak and when to stay silent, when to open our heart to another and when to engage in polite conversation. And we respect another's right not to know, to be caught in illusion, to follow the path of his or her own desires. Freedom is also the freedom to make mistakes, to go wrong. We never judge, because we respect the right of each person to pursue her own destiny, to lose herself again and again. Sometimes we are allowed to point out the way, to give another a helping hand. Instinctively our heart opens and we allow ourself to be used. But we have to be very careful that we not get attached to this work, that it not gratify our own ego. Otherwise the love cannot flow freely, and help easily becomes an imposition. To limit another's freedom, to deny another's right to choose his or her own path, is to put ourself above God who gave us this freedom.

Once the ego becomes too involved, we lose the guidance and protection we are given. Caught in the grip of the ego, even a "spiritual ego," we remain within its sphere of illusion. Following our own desires, how-ever well-meaning, we veil ourself from the light that guides and protects us. In the sphere of the ego we are dependent upon ourself. Surrendering our ego in the arena of real servanthood, we are dependent upon our master. Only then can we fully participate in life with-out the risk of getting caught in its illusions.

THE DYNAMIC OF SPEED

Our prayers and spiritual aspirations call down the grace that creates a container of protection on the inner planes to help us do our work in the world safely. But protection is also given through the dynamic of speed. On the spiri-tual path the wayfarer is "speeded up." Darkness is denser than light; greed is slower than love. Selfless service moves at a quicker vibration than patterns of desire. The Self is much faster than the ego.

The speed of our devotion protects us from the slower energies of ego-desires because these denser energies do not stick to us. We are not so easily caught in their nega-tive patterns. If something is spinning at a certain speed it throws off negative or denser thought-forms, emotions, or other energies that might stick to it. The speed of our inner vibration creates a vortex of light and love that in itself protects us. This vortex is always around us, and it increases when our devotion is more focused, when our heart is more full of longing.

Speed allows us to avoid many of the pitfalls that surround us: we are moving too fast to be drawn into their negative vortex. Speed also enables us to change directions more quickly when we encounter situations or energy patterns that could distract or damage us. It

enables us to be more flexible and less rigid, less identified with any pattern or form.

Through an awareness of life as a dynamic flow of
energy, we can see the importance of speed: how it can
enable us to move from situation to situation more quickly and be more fluid in our response to any change. The
energy patterns of life are continually changing, and the
quicker we are able to respond to their changes the more
dynamically we can participate in life.

Through our inner effort and the practices of the
path, we can free ourself of many of the burdens that slow
us down: the unnecessary possessions that cling to us,
the attachments that sap our energy. Most people are
unaware of how their accumulation of possessions burdens them inwardly, draining their energy. Unused or
unnecessary possessions are a particular burden; they are
like a dead weight. The physical plane is the most dense
and slow-moving, and if our attention is focused on this
plane by too many possessions, we become inwardly
constricted. Our attachments always draw our energy.

The mystic learns to travel light, to have only what is
needed. This does not mean that we live as ascetics;
in our Western culture this also creates obstacles. For
example, in many parts of America it is necessary to have
a car; otherwise one cannot participate easily in life and
may even become a burden to others. We live according
to the need of the time and are "unattached to ways and
means." This is the practice of the poverty of the heart.

Burdens and attachments exist on different levels.
Our physical possessions may be the most visible, but
emotional attachments can be very draining. Knowledge can also be a burden as it keeps our minds caught
within its parameters. The mystic needs to use the knowledge that is needed but be free of mental patterns that
could constrict her. As long as we are not attached to any

body of knowledge, we can use it and then put it behind us. We learn not to identify ourself with anything but our Beloved.

Spiritual attachments also drain our energy and create a barrier on the inner plane. Patterns of identity form very easily and become a protection against the unknown and the energy of chaos. The mystic who is prepared to live on the borders of the unknown has become familiar with chaos. So many times we have seen our own limited sense of self destroyed by the energy of the path, by the faster dynamic of His love for us. The Sufi master Bhai Sahib said of his house, "This is a place of drunkards and a place of change." The dynamic and intoxicating energy of divine love frees us again and again, helping us to step outside the patterns that so quickly form around us. Only when we are free of our attachments and self-created patterns can we fully respond to His hint, can we catch the thread of His unfolding love.

On the Sufi path this thread is finally all we have to hold us; it is a state of both vulnerability and total protection. The wayfarer is taken through the stage of *fanâ* (annihilation), in which all attachments, both inner and outer, fall away and the very structure of the ego is changed. This leads to the state of *baqâ* (permanence), in which we inwardly abide only with God:

> The Sufi master al-Kharqanî was asked, "Who is the appropriate person to speak about *fanâ* and *baqâ?*" He answered, "That is knowledge for the one who is suspended by a silk thread from the heavens to the earth when a big cyclone comes and takes all trees, houses, and mountains and throws them in the ocean until it fills the ocean. If that cyclone is unable to move him who is hanging

by the silk thread, then he is the one who can speak on *fanâ* and *baqâ*."

The more we are free of our attachments, the more fully we are able to give ourself to the flow of life, whose energy takes us where we need to be. The energy of life then supports us, even our burdens. In the words of the Sufi master Bhai Sahib, "You float in the river and let your burdens float beside you." Certain resistances, insecurities, doubts, and fears will always remain. They are a part of our physiological, emotional, and mental make-up. We are not intended to be perfect. But life carries them with us; they become part of the eddies and flows of life's current. They do not interfere with our journey or the work we need to do.

Unfortunately, one of the effects of our cultural focus on the transcendent aspect of the divine has been a pre-occupation with perfection. In heaven perfection does exist, but not on this physical plane of manifestation. If we aspire to live in heaven we will try to be perfect. If we aspire to live our divinity here on earth we will accept our imperfections, knowing that they are part of a greater wholeness. If we are to fully embrace the mystery of in-carnation, we have to leave behind our longing to be perfect, our desire for heaven. In the words of al-Ansarî,

> Strive to be the true human being:
> one who knows love, one who knows pain.[1]

THE FLOW OF LIFE AND THE TAO

Working with the energy of life, we do not impose our will, but neither do we stand aside from our responsibilities. We are a part of life and actively participate in its unfolding. Through learning to work with the flow of life and its patterns of energy, we are able to avoid unnecessary obstacles and difficulties. And when there are difficulties that need to be faced, we work with them carefully, according to their nature. This is the ancient Chinese wisdom of the Tao, as illustrated in Chuang Tzu's story of the master carver. Cook Ting explained to Lord Wen how he mastered his skill:

> What your servant loves best is the Tao, which is better than any art. When I started to cut up oxen, what I saw was the complete ox.... Now I see the natural lines and my knife slides through the great hollows, follows the natural cavities, using that which is already there to my advantage. Thus, I miss the great sinews and even more so, the great bones. A good cook changes his knife annually, because he slices. An ordinary cook has to change his knife every month, because he hacks. Now this knife of mine I have been using for nineteen years, and it has cut thousands of oxen. However, its blade is as sharp as if it had been sharpened. Between the joints there are spaces, and the blade of the knife has no real thickness. If you put what has no real thickness into spaces such as these there is plenty of room to move around, certainly enough for the knife to work through. However, when I come to a difficult part and can see that it will be difficult, I take care and pay due regard. I look carefully and I move with caution. Then, very gently, I move the knife until there is a parting and the flesh falls apart like a lump of earth falling to the ground. I stand with the knife in my hand looking around and then, with an air of satisfaction, I wipe the knife and put it away.

"Splendid!" said Lord Wen Hui. "I have heard what cook Ting has to say and from his words I have learned how to live fully."[2]

Cook Ting learned to see the natural lines, to go into the spaces, and to work with what is already there. He avoided many difficulties, and worked carefully when he encountered obstacles. According to the Taoist masters this is how to "live fully," how to engage in life without imposing, how to allow things to take their course. They allowed for the imperfections in life and were friends with confusion. They recognized the importance of flexibility and that knowing when to stop averts trouble. They held the primal wisdom of working with the flow of life.

The Tao is the energy of life that flows everywhere and is present in all things. To work with the Tao is to be in harmony with the whole, and with the movement and unfolding of the whole. We are not separate from life, but a part of it. Only if we recognize this natural wholeness can we participate in life not as an outsider, but as part of the Tao. Then life nourishes itself through us. Life uses us according to our true nature, and helps us to live this true nature which is in harmony with the whole. Living in accord with the Tao is imaged in the *Tao Te Ching*:

> There may be an arsenal of weapons,
> but nobody ever uses them.
> People enjoy their food,
> take pleasure in being with their families,
> spend week-ends working in their gardens,
> delight in the doings of the neighborhood.[3]

Once we step outside of the whole we become a stranger in our own world. The world becomes complicated and unbalanced; we no longer know how to live in harmony with ourself and our environment. But we can return to our inborn state of oneness, not as a child in the bliss of unknowing, but as a mature person who, aware of his limitations, recognizes that there is a wisdom that can live through him. This is the primal wisdom of the Tao, when to stop in order to avert trouble, when to avoid obstacles that we do not need to confront. If we can reconnect with the simplicity of our own self, in which this deeper knowing is hidden, life will teach us what it needs: how to regain its balance and heal itself. Then we can return to the ways of oneness in which all are given what they need:

> Be content with what you have;
> rejoice in the ways things are.
> When you realize there is nothing lacking,
> the whole world belongs to you.[4]

LIFE'S NATURAL PROTECTION

We have forgotten the essential knowledge that life is a self-regulating wholeness, a living organism of which we are a part. When we relate to life as an adversary, we constellate our own patterns of defense against its natural energy, and protect ourself against the very thing we need to nourish us: the wholeness and flow of life.

If we alter our attitude toward life, we will discover that real security comes from an inner alignment with life, a knowing that we are a part of life and its continual regeneration. This is not a security that will protect us from life's changes, but one that will support and carry us through the difficulties and times of confusion that are a natural element of its flow. Life is not meant to be static, but a continual movement that takes us through the stages of our own development, offering us new perspectives and possibilities. Life that becomes static or defined leaves us in a backwater that stagnates and becomes polluted. A different sense of security comes from being part of the flow, because only then are we supported by life's momentum, carried along by the current. And the more we give ourself to life, the more life responds by giving us what we need.

A process of separation from the instinctual world may have given us a certain degree of autonomy and helped the development of consciousness, but it has alienated us from our own life. Our masculine drive for the control of our instinctual nature has created a culture where parents have to read books about how to love and care for their children. Because we do not trust life, we do not allow life to protect and care for us.

The darkness of life, the fear of violence and deprivation, are real. We cannot ignore their presence. Only she who has nothing left to lose, the idiot or the saint, dares to leave her door always open. Like the master carver, we can combine conscious discrimination with a respect for life's natural lines. If we allow life to guide us, we will realize a natural dynamic of self-preservation, a deep respect for life itself, and the knowing that we are "the sons and daughters of life's longing for itself."

This shift of consciousness is so profound it will take time to engage. But we can no longer afford to focus on our personal well-being. Those who have experienced a reality beyond the ego need to lead the way, for once we have stepped beyond the ego we have glimpsed the vaster wholeness that nourishes and supports us.

For the Sufi, "Only that which cannot be lost in a shipwreck is ours." And in a shipwreck one can lose everything, even one's own life. This is the freedom of the mystic who knows that the only real security comes from the thin thread of love that runs between the worlds, the bond of "He loves them and they love Him." This thread that is found within the heart is also woven into the fabric of the world. Here the care and protection we need are always present, a care and protection that are not imposed but a part of life. We may not always be saved from apparent disasters, which may have come to free us. But we are protected from the greater danger of cutting ourself off from our life and our own soul and having to live in the shadowlands of a world without His presence.

The mystic does not walk blindly, but uses the light of His love and the consciousness of discrimination to go with the flow of life. The name of God is one of the greatest protections for the wayfarer, because it directly connects us to Him whose name we call. I was once told a moving story by a woman who had been teaching English in prison and fallen in love with a prisoner who had real talent at writing. When he was released she married him, but he could not escape his attraction to drugs. One day he took her for a drive in the countryside, and stopping the car, pulled a gun from his pocket. She realized that he was crazed with cocaine and for some paranoid reason thought that she had betrayed him. He pointed the gun at her and she knew that he would pull the trigger. She could not fight him, and in her desperation called out "Allâh." In that instant his expression changed, and sorrow replaced his wild anger. He handed her the gun and asked for her forgiveness.

Knowing that the world belongs to God, the mystic is able to leave behind many of the burdens of security that those who do not know Him seem to require. We are able to "travel light" and thus respond to the real need of the time without the constrictions that come from self-concern. We also come to know the strength and power of His love for us as a living presence that dissolves our fears and helps us to see the light in every recess of His world. We discover that even when we feel most alone, He is with us, hidden, invisible, but always present.

Life needs us to be free and responsive so that we can bring His love into the marketplace. If we recognize His oneness and repeat His name, He cannot turn away from us. The doors of His mercy are always open. The mystic no longer needs to protect himself against life. Those who are in service to Him have been given an energy that will protect them from any darkness that will interfere with this work. This energy is already present both within us and in the world. It is a part of the quality of joy that is awakening within life.

Joy

"I have no name:
I am but two days old."
What shall I call thee?
"I happy am,
Joy is my name."
Sweet joy befall thee!

William Blake [1]

THE NATURAL JOY OF LIFE

Joy is present in every atom of creation, waiting to be activated by God's love in His world. Joy is a living remembrance of God, an affirmation of His oneness in the midst of life. Without joy life remains mundane and colorless, defined only by its battles for survival and dominance. Joy is like a sip of the wine of remembrance that intoxicates the soul with the awareness of His presence, a presence that is not separate from life but is the core of every activity, every passing moment.

The idea that God is other than life abandons the world to His absence. Then we are left alone, and the world holds only the pursuits of pleasure, the shadows of our real need for Him. But the lover knows how the awakening of love brings joy to life, makes every leaf radiant with color. She has experienced how every moment can carry a quality of intoxication. The world comes alive in love and gives us a glimpse of another dimension in which the heart always sings and the real colors of creation are visible.

Life has so many colors, just as it has so many hidden meanings. Awakening to love, we awaken to life in a different way; we see, smell, taste, and touch its hidden promise. Love lifts the veils that separate us from our Beloved, and reveals the wonder and glory of His world. For the lover even time loses its fixed quality; its boundaries dissolve as a moment lasts forever, as a kiss intoxicates us with the bliss that belongs to the soul.

Yes, we return from these moments into a harsher world, where lovers part and love's taste becomes bitter. The bleak lines of the world break through again, and we feel the abandonment of a world without our lover's presence, without his touch or smell. And yet, once we have sipped this wine, we know somewhere what is waiting. Our days may become dull again, and with the mechanical motions of life we pass the time, but we can never fully forget when love touched us and its sweet joy was present.

We cannot quantify joy. It slips through our fingers and runs down the street laughing at us. Unexpectedly it may come to us, like a jester, joking at our seriousness. It makes fun of the way we look to the future for fulfillment, because it knows that only the moment is real. Joy has no ladder to climb, no advancement to pursue. It has no prospects, and it is not given or taken away. It does not care for our well-being because it is our well-being.

Sometimes, in our dreams, we are able to slip past the guardians of common sense and allow ourself a taste of joy. Within a dream's endless moment we are again in this landscape of promise. Our dreams open this door and offer us what we long for. This is the soul speaking to us, reminding us, giving us its secret sustenance to carry into life. But so often we wake to watch the magic fade into the busyness of our day, and wonder if it was ever real, if it will ever return.

The mystic knows that this natural joy is not lost, is not a dream, but a reality that is accessible, even though no roads lead there. And the poet recaptures these moments for us, the luminous dream that is always present, the childhood of the imagination in which laughter is echoing. We feel how something which one cannot make happen unexpectedly happens, how something dead becomes alive. In the words of E. E. Cummings:

> (i who have died am alive again today,
> and this is the sun's birthday;this is the birth
> day of life and of love and wings:and of the gay
> great happening illimitably earth)
>
> how should tasting touching hearing seeing
> breathing any—lifted from the no
> of all nothing—human merely being
> doubt unimaginable You?
>
> (now the ears of my ears awake and
> now the eyes of my eyes are opened) [2]

Joy is life that is awake and alive, brimming with possibilities—the possibilities that belong to its source in the infinite. Joy is the impossible that springs from the mundane. One may call it a miracle, but it is really a natural occurrence that is given again and again. It is just the moment that is lived, that is alive.

Joy is full of promise but has no bargaining potential. Joy does not belong to anyone, nor does it offer security. There is no hierarchy of joy, no position of power. It cannot be packaged, and there is no real substitute for joy. It is a quality of the soul that belongs to life, and is too free for the mind to grasp and imprison. You cannot regulate joy. It is either present or absent. When you feel joy you are fully alive, and without joy there is no song to be heard, no music in the air. Life becomes an existence rather than a celebration, and loses its own vitality and creative potential.

And now life is dying. We have lived too long without joy. Although materially we have everything we need, life is beginning to forget its own need to celebrate, to be intoxicated, to be in love. Life is beginning to forget its own source, the infinite of which it is an expression.

The power of our thought has defined life to such a degree that life itself responds to our patterns of definition. We are not aware of the power of our thought, how it affects the life around us. We do not realize how the thought-forms of humanity influence the world, how the world reflects our desires and aspirations, as well as our fears and failings. And because we do not live with joy, because we deny it in ourselves, it is being lost from our world.

Yet we do not even notice. We are too busy to be aware of what we are doing. Even those who sincerely try to help humanity or save the environment often approach their work with the same thought-patterns that caused the sickness. The world was never a problem to be solved, and it certainly does not need any imposed pattern of salvation. The world is a magical, dynamically changing dance of which we are a part.

How can we bring joy back to life and to the world? By simply saying "yes" to our own divinity, to our own soul, to the oneness of which we are a part. Life is longing to reveal itself to us, to make itself known, to show us the patterns of its dance. But it cannot do this without our participation, without our partnership. And to deny the divinity of life is like tearing the heart out of a person and saying, "Now live!"

We are busy with our salvation, whether material, spiritual, or ecological. But why do we need to be saved or salvaged? Are we a piece of wreckage or an expression of wonder? To whom do we belong? If we belong to ourself then there is much salvation to be accomplished, much wreckage to be redeemed. But if we belong to our Beloved, whose hands created us, then whose hands can heal our wounds? Who can give us joy again?

THE JOY OF SERVICE

If we think that God is separate from us, we are left alone with our own problems. He remains in heaven, and we remain abandoned with ourselves. Alone, we shoulder the burdens of an empty world, thinking we have control of our own life, forgetting the basic principle that everything is His will. We think that we rule our world, even though the signs around us indicate our impotence. We cannot even master ourselves, our own desires, our own greed.

The mystic knows that "no one knows God but God," and that "He is beyond even our idea of the beyond." But we have also experienced His nearness; we know that "He is closer to you than your very neck vein." He is the cry of the sick and the laughter of the child. He is the rain drenching the meadows. Even our own longing is His longing for Himself. There is nothing other than He.

We live with the paradox that He is other than we and yet we know that He is one. In love's oneness "I am He whom I love; He whom I love is me." But we are always His servant and He our Lord. The servant is never the Lord. The attitude of servanthood protects us from the dangers of inflation that come from the experience of oneness.[3] And yet our station as servant brings us close to our Beloved. The true servant belongs to his Master and is always attentive to His need. The more we

are attentive to His needs, the more closely our consciousness is aligned with Him, and the more our heart
is attuned to Him. In our servanthood we leave behind
the veils of the ego as we look to our Master.

In order for us to fully serve Him, the consciousness
of the heart needs to be awakened, because only through
the consciousness of the heart can we know the needs of
our Beloved. And the consciousness of the heart is a
state of oneness. In the words of Ibn 'Arabî, "Union is
the very secret of servanthood." [4]

The mystic embraces the paradox of union and
separation: the immersion in love's oneness that leads to
true servanthood. In our service is our joy. There is no
deeper joy than to serve the Beloved. Then the heart
sings the song of belonging, and we are able to fulfill
our deepest purpose: to be here for Him. Nothing is of
greater meaning to the servant than to serve her Lord;
nothing is more fulfilling for the lover than to meet the
needs of her Beloved.

The lover who looks to her Beloved cares only for
His needs. And the needs of the Beloved embrace all of
His creation. However it may appear, nothing is excluded.
Too often we only see the darkness that covers the face
of the world, the suffering and sadness of humanity. This
suffering is real and requires our awareness and compas-
sion. But when the servant sees with the eyes of her
Master, a different picture emerges, in which care and
love are revealed. Associating the divine with paradise
and perfection, we blind ourselves to the way His oneness works in the world, how His hidden touch cleanses
the heart. We associate the darkness of the world with
the absence of God, unaware that the forces of creation
have a deeper purpose than superficial happiness.

The lover knows that pain and love walk hand in
hand, that the rose bush has both a thorn and a fragrant

flower. We know how sorrow can open the heart more quickly than kindness. Darkness and light are not the opposites they appear, but part of the mystery of how He hides and reveals Himself. One of His secrets is that in the midst of darkness there is always a point of pure light, just as His light holds the secret of His darkness. Once we step away from the polarity of opposites, we can glimpse the deeper purpose of humanity and be in service to this purpose. This was the prayer of the Prophet: "Show us, Lord, everything just as it really is."[5]

JOY AND LAUGHTER

The doors to oneness have been opened and the attitude of inner attention and service welcomes us inside. In the oneness of servanthood a joy is waiting to be lived. Those who give themselves in service to oneness will rediscover this joy, which also gives them protection. Joy protects us from negative thought-forms, from desires and patterns of restriction. Joy belongs to the profusion of life, to its ever-flowing source. It continually nourishes us with life's essence, while its dancing energy scatters the energies that could constrict, disturb, or attack us.

Joy is too quick for the mind to follow or for its doubts to dispel. Joy knows no arguments and cannot be possessed. Joy is given, lived, enjoyed. It cannot be limited by any form, because it does not belong to form. It belongs to the moment the formless flow of life comes into manifestation, before it is caught in any pattern of conditioning. It is life's constant abundance and sings the blessing of the Creator.

Joy *is*, and the continual completeness of joy reminds us that we *are*. The experience of joy is an experience of our own essential nature, before "time held us dying." Young children who are free of time's constrictions, who can live forever in each moment, have a closer connection to life and joy. They are carefree in the simplicity of their own self and the wonder of life. This is the quality of life we need to reawaken, but with the awareness of adults who know how precious such simplicity and wonder are, and how each moment is an opportunity to remember Him and praise Him. Joy is an expression of wonder, and it reminds us of life's secret: that "He who was a hidden treasure wanted to be known, and so He created the world." In the joy of life we can feel the presence of this "hidden treasure." Joy can open us to life as it really is.

Joy is full of laughter, like the moment Blake expresses in his poem, *Laughing Song,*

> When the green woods laugh with the voice of joy,
> And the dimpling stream runs laughing by;
> And the air does laugh with our merry wit,
> And the green hill laughs with the noise of it.[6]

Joy and laughter belong together, a dance that takes us out of ourself into a simple world that is often obscured. So easily we get caught in our preoccupations that we forget this laughter of being alive, a joy that we share with all of life. And for the mystic there is also the deeper laughter that recognizes the absurdity of so much of what we think is important. This is the humor of the Sufi figure Nasruddin, as in the following story:

> Nasruddin was riding his donkey one day when it was frightened by something on its path and began to run very quickly. He couldn't manage to hold his donkey back, and some farmers yelled out,

"Nasruddin, what's the hurry? Why are you going so fast?"

"Don't ask me," he shouted back. "Ask my donkey!"

These stories deflate our self-importance, and open us to the laughter that sees life "upside down" and often present a truer picture. This is also the laughter of our dreams, those that play with us and our preconceptions. One friend dreamed that the end of the world was coming, and everyone was escaping by spaceship:

> Somehow I am left behind, or my spaceship does not work. I am left alone at the end of the world. I walk away from the launch pad. Then I come to where the end of the world is, and discover that it is in fact the end of a week-long intensive marketing campaign by a large department store. The sales girls are sitting with their feet up and shoes off, having a cup of coffee, saying what an intense week it has been.

Because he could not escape, the dreamer discovers that the world he knew was in fact a "week-long intensive marketing campaign by a large department store." Suddenly the tragedy of being left alone at the end of the world falls away as the dance of appearances reveals its joke. The sight of the sales girls of life's illusions, servants of the goddess *Maya*, sitting with their feet up and their shoes off, frees the dreamer of much of the apparent seriousness of the world.

How often does the Sufi master have a twinkle in his eyes, a smile hidden behind his beard, as he watches his disciples become caught in appearances, taking too seriously the eternal play of *maya*? Both the material and spiritual world offer a myriad of deceptions. But if we can laugh at ourselves, at how often we are deceived and caught, then we can throw aside our own self-importance and discover a place of joy and freedom behind this façade of self-importance. In the words of one Sufi teacher, "Nothing matters very much and even that does not matter very much."

FREEDOM AND LOVE'S ENDLESS HORIZON

Laughter, like freedom, is bought at a price, and the mystic knows that the only real price is ourself. One of the dangers of the path is to take oneself too seriously. Then one can never have access to the joke of creation, to the humor that ripples through this dance of appearances. Laughing at ourself, we are able to strip away some of the coverings that blind us. In the light we can see that the darkness is not as it seems, and that even in the greatest suffering the soul is cared for with infinite tenderness.

As human beings we are caught between the opposites of suffering and happiness, instinctively turning away from suffering and pursuing happiness. Yet the wayfarer is one who seeks to be free of the pull of the opposites, knowing that there is a deeper oneness in which all opposites are combined. Although we do not seek suffering, we aspire not to reject any offering of our Beloved, knowing that real freedom only comes through accepting our destiny—drinking the cup of life with both hands. To reject part of what life brings us is to reject the essential unity of our Beloved.

Freedom is the song of the soul that walks into the arena of life with her head high. We know that there will be pain and joy. To deny one is to exclude the other. If we cut life into pieces it loses its music. In this bargain we also lose our power, because the true power of a human being belongs to our wholeness, our need for darkness as well as light. This is not the power of domination, but of affirmation: the power to say "yes" to life in all its contradictions, in its abundance and destitution. We need this power if we are to step outside the limited parameters of our defined life and embrace the vaster totality of which we are a part. And yet this power is only given to us when we make this step. We cannot have access to it before we make the commitment to life in its wholeness.

There is no guarantee that we will find what we seek, that our prayers will be answered, that our suffering will diminish. The lover does not have any insurance except the craving for love, the helplessness of her own need. But once we say "yes" to this journey and the shore slips away behind us, we will find that we are drawn into a current that has been flowing since the beginning of time. This current defines our journey. Sometimes we may have to take out our oars and row past rocks, calling out in prayer and supplication. Or when the wind comes we can put up the sail of our devotion that effortlessly carries us. There will also be days, months, maybe years when we seem becalmed and cut off from the current of love. But even when nothing appears to happen, the journey continues, taking us further than our imaginings. And there is much laughter at the craziness of this quest, this reckless giving of ourself.

Do we need to know where we are going, to have a map in our hand? Would we even understand the strange hieroglyphs that describe the course of this journey? Or are our laughter and longing enough to carry us beyond the horizon of the ego, into the vastness of our real nature? Yes, there are dangers, some real and many self-created. There are whirlpools and storms, and there are sunsets of dazzling beauty and nighttimes soft and silent, with the stars falling into our hands.

There is no purpose to this journey, because any purpose would be too narrow a definition. Instead there is an endless giving of ourself, a dying to the known. Again and again we are made and remade, thrown into the torrents that undo us, the silence that deepens us, the love that melts us. Sometimes we wash up on strange shores, or seem to drown, lost and forgotten. At different stages on this journey some travelers hold back, unable or unwilling to give of themselves any more, to be ship-wrecked yet again. And so they set up shop at their last port of call, and tell stories of their journey. But other voyagers are drawn always further, not caring what happens to them. Their loving cannot cease; their destiny would laugh at any limit. The journey is ever onward, demanding, exhilarating, until one day we realize that we are the ocean itself, and each sunrise and sunset reflects upon the waters of our being. Then the joy of the soul is given to all of creation as love finally claims us for its own.

Magic

God is alive. Magic is afoot.

Leonard Cohen

THE NATURE OF MAGIC

Our culture has lost its understanding of magic and ex-
iled its magicians. Where are those who can awaken us
to the dance of creation and to the names of God that are
woven into the texture of everyday life? Who can take
the colors of this dance and spin robes of joy, then pass
them out on street corners to tired and unsuspecting
workers? Sadly, we have banished magic to the realm of
entertainment, where magicians deceive us with sleight
of hand or a trick of mirrors, as they pull rabbits out of
hats or disappear in a cloud of smoke. Or we reduce magic
to storybook worlds of witches and wizards, who make
spells and potions to acquire treasures or battle dragons.

But real magic is something else entirely, and is rarely
practiced in the visible world. Magic is primarily the use
of energy from a different level of reality, and it can be
used to infuse this world with the infinite possibilities of
other dimensions. Magic usually concerns the manipulation of the energy patterns behind creation; it subtly
alters the force fields of life so that certain events can
take place or certain energies can be released. Magic is
available to us all if we know where to look and what to
hope for.

Of course there is dark as well as good magic. Dark
magic works with energy patterns for personal gain or
power. Good magic helps humanity. And there are many
different levels of magic. Some magic affects only single

individuals, maybe to make a small difference in their lives, while higher magic might concern a community, even the whole of humanity and the course of world events. There is also magic directly related to helping our spiritual evolution. This magic involves creating an atmosphere in which we can connect with our higher nature more easily, and thus consciously realize and live our divinity.

Every spiritual path works with energy patterns, bringing a higher energy closer to consciousness so that its practitioners can have access to and work with it. A spiritual community or retreat center is in itself an energy field, creating a container of peace, devotion, love, or selfless service, depending on the energy of the path. Entering a spiritual center or community, one can feel the quality of the energy that belongs to its particular lineage. While some evoke a feeling of detachment, others might resonate more with the heart and the feeling of love. The energy field of a particular path affects all those who come into contact with it, helping align them with the spiritual qualities of that path. In the light created by a spiritual community, we can have easier and greater access to our own light. A spiritual community is also beneficial to the surrounding environment, including the people, plants, and animals nearby.

Every person has her own natural magic that affects her surroundings. Learning to work with one's own natural magic is part of the teaching of a spiritual path. Mostly this teaching is kept hidden, even from the practitioner, so that it cannot be used for personal gain. But there are also occasions when it needs to be known, when we need to consciously reclaim this part of our heritage.

When we recognize that life is an interrelated web of light and darkness, we can begin to understand how our own energy field affects not only our immediate surroundings, but how it affects the whole. The flow of energy that radiates from each of us directly influences the energy field of life. Light attracts light, darkness draws darkness to itself. And just as we have our own individual energy blocks, so are there blocks in the energy fields of life. Working with these energy blocks has always been a part of the spiritual work of the masters of love, and they train their disciples to help them in this work. The power of love and devotion, combined with an understanding of the energy patterns of creation—the ways energy flows throughout humanity and all of life—can help unblock restricted energy. Then light and love, wisdom and meaning can be more accessible. Individuals and communities can have greater and easier access to their divine nature.

There are specific techniques for working with the energy patterns of love, and exact laws that must be followed. For example, one is not allowed to influence a person against his or her free will. Also, one must not release too much light at any one time. Too much light can throw someone off balance, even make her crazy, as the veils that contained her sense of self are dissolved. In the words of T.S. Eliot, "human kind cannot bear very much reality."[1] The veils of our ego give us our identity; even our psychological problems and blocks help to define us.

Yet there is a way to work behind the scenes of life, just as one can work within the hearts of people, to gently and gradually dissolve the blocks and barriers that prevent people from realizing and living who they really are. There is a way to subtly shift the veils of illusion so that we can come to see ourself reflected more clearly, so that we can glimpse the deeper purpose of our life more easily. This is real magic, and it will help the world and everything in it come alive again with its own magic.

THE COLORS OF MAGIC

Magic is always present. Without magic the world would lose all its color and vibrancy, all its tricks and surprises. And yet we have forgotten the presence of magic. Just as we have forgotten that the world belongs to God, so we have abandoned ourself to a world without magic in which we see life only through the veils of our own limitations and inadequacies. Lost in this forgetting, we experience our life as just a dull succession of days, "a walking shadow...signifying nothing."

But magic is around every corner, waiting to be lived, waiting to be welcomed. We can bend the prison bars and escape from our conditioning, from our limited perception of ourself and our world. Magic brings the promise of springtime when it should be winter. Magic connects us to the light in the cells of our body, and spins these cells with joy and laughter. Magic sometimes makes mischief, when we take ourself too seriously, when we limit our freedom. Like Puck in *A Midsummer Night's Dream*, our magical self puts a potion on our sleeping eyes, inverting all our values and awakening us to love. Magic brings together the different worlds, weaving a sacred texture out of dreams and starlight.

Magic can make us alive in different ways, help us to sing and dance the mystery and wonder of our divinity. The natural world is full of simple magic, the way a flower follows the sun, a salmon finds its way home, but our sophistication has excluded us from the simple miracles of life. Magic is all around us, and we can use it to wake ourselves up in a world that includes and nourishes us, stimulates and excites us.

When the prescribed rules of our physical world become infused with the qualities of a different dimension, life can finally be itself, laughingly responding with its natural sense of limitless possibilities and infinite surprises. We may have defined and categorized our visible world, but do we know what happens when the invisible is made visible, when rainbows guide us to real pots of gold? When we traded our shamans for scientists we abandoned a whole spectrum of existence, lost an entire realm of experience.

We do not even recognize the beings of light or the shadows of darkness that permeate our physical world. We do not know how to speak to angels or welcome them into our presence. Even nature spirits have become just creatures of children's books. We have banished so many worlds and are left only with a vacuum we attempt to fill with material pleasure. What would happen if we became awake again to worlds made of light and colors, if we sacrificed the security of our defined knowledge for dimensions that are not defined by physical touch? Why should only initiates have access to the inner worlds?

There might be both beauty and horror waiting, but we have excluded ourself from what is possible for too long. Human beings have access to many different levels of reality. That is how we are made. The mystic has long walked in fields of love, in landscapes of devotion, in places where the invisible and the visible meet and merge, from where miracles happen. We have been given glimpses of realities that are not limited to what we can see with our physical eyes, touch with our physical hands. As the innocent fool Bottom, in *A Midsummer Night's Dream*, wisely reported after his venture into fairyland:

> I have had a most rare vision. I have had a dream past the wit of man to say what dream it was.... The eye of man hath not heard, the ear of man hath not seen, man's hand is not able to taste, his tongue to conceive, nor his heart to report,

what my dream was…it shall be called "Bottom's Dream" because it has no bottom.[2]

But does this have to remain a dream, accessible only to "the lunatic, the lover and the poet"? Can we not reclaim our magical heritage, along with our divine knowing?

When the Puritans banned the maypole dancing, one of the last vestiges of communal magic was lost. The somber-colored Puritans saw its dance as immoral, and maybe by then all that remained was the fun and sexuality of a fertility ritual. But the roots of such rituals belong to an era when magic was part of everyday life, when the spirits were alive and Puck was not just a figure in a play. Our rational minds replaced the potency of magic with the label "superstition," and the door to other worlds was closed. But we are now entering an era when these doors are opening, when magic is needed to awaken us to our multidimensional nature. The dances of the different worlds need to merge and flow together, like the ribbons on the maypole dance—the many hues of His love for us. This world is not just a mirror of light and dark, but a kaleidoscope of interwoven energies that each reflect a different quality of His oneness.

So why do we deny magic? Is it just the conditioning of rationalism, or, like the patriarchal fathers, are we frightened of a world we cannot understand, cannot control? Are we wary that magic might make mischief with our life, turn it upside down? But in the absence of real magic we are left starving for anything that will surprise and disorient us, sweep us away from our limited and constricted lives. We long to fall in love, to surrender our sensible self into the unexpected and dreamlike world of romance. These are the images that haunt our screens and imagination—this is the magic that we long for.

But why should magic be limited to romantic love? Why can't it be present at the breakfast table, and in the workplace? Do we need to split our lives into fragments rather than live the wholeness of being human? The maypole dancers did not keep magic only for holidays. The dance gave color to the mundanity of daily life. The other world was always close by, even when it made mischief.

WORKING WITH THE MAGIC OF LIFE

There are many levels of magic, just as there are different levels of reality. The lowest level of magic is the manipulation of matter: using one's mind to bend a fork or spoon, for example. Focusing on the image of something you desire until it manifests in your life is another form of magic. Consciously or unconsciously creating patterns of emotional dependency either in individuals or a group dynamic is a negative form of magic. Higher forms of magic include using energy from the inner worlds to heal someone, or create a sacred space in which the divine is more accessible.

One of the highest levels of magic is the awakening of divine oneness that is being given to humanity. A more complete level of awareness is being made accessible to ordinary consciousness. A veil is being lifted to help humanity remember its real nature. This shift has a "ripple effect" as a higher energy permeates a denser plane of consciousness. Part of this shift is to make accessible certain secrets of creation that until now have been hidden. As the patterns of creation, the energy flow of life, become visible, so will we be given access to the way to work with these energy patterns. Not only the consciousness of oneness, but other knowledge is also being made known. An aspect of this knowledge has begun to surface in various fields of "energy work" and psycho-spiritual techniques, but the limitation of this present knowledge is that it focuses on the healing or development of individuals. This keeps the knowledge within the parameters of the previous age, and so denies its real potential. Working with energy fields should infuse the whole of the outer world, all of life, with the dynamic energy of the inner planes. The moment an individual focuses on her own development, a certain magic is lost, certain colors cannot penetrate our thought-forms.

When we work with the magic of life, it is essential to perceive life as a continually moving interdependent whole. Only then can our consciousness become attuned to the energy patterns within creation. When our consciousness is attuned in this way we will see how to work with this dynamic flow, how our consciousness can affect the way life manifests. For example, one spiritual technique is to imprint one of the divine names, or a sacred phrase, into the energy of creation before it manifests. This directly aligns creation with the Creator and makes the manifest world more fully charged with the energy of His presence. Different divine names can be given to different energy patterns, helping His qualities to flow into the world. For the Sufi His greatest name, Allâh, can help align all of creation with His divine unity, both His immanent and His transcendent nature.

Magic can also alter the veils of perception so that certain divine qualities—beauty, joy, grandeur, etc.— become more visible, more directly accessible within our experience. Aligning the inner and outer worlds in this way can enable humanity to have more clear access to its higher nature, and thus enact its higher purpose more directly. It will also enable the energy and meaning of the inner world to flow more freely into everyday life. The inner world can then manifest in outer events that more directly embody our higher purpose, and can also influence our ability to read the signs of life, the way the outer world reflects and makes conscious our purpose.

Magic can help us see the patterns of life more clearly and show us how to work with these patterns. While work in the outer world usually involves physical or mental effort, work in the inner world requires awareness and attention. Meditation and other spiritual practices help us develop these abilities, open our awareness and keep a focused attention.

Just as we work with energy blocks in our body or psyche, so can we learn to work with the energy blocks in our workplace or community. For example, spiritual communities often get stuck when collective shadow dynamics block the flow of dedication and create doubts. There is a way to work with these blocks on the inner planes before they affect the well-being of the community and its spiritual integrity. Sometimes a few words need to be said, not directed at "solving the problem" but at more subtly releasing the flow. This can also be done with music or movement. Sometimes the trickster energy, as imaged in the Sufi figure of Nasruddin, is most effective, bringing laughter and turning a situation upside down. For the Sufi such work is never imposed—people are always left free to live in the darkness of their discontent—but there are many different ways to disentangle a potential problem and allow love and aspiration to flow more freely.

Seeing only the outer world, we do not notice difficulties until they constellate. As the inner world becomes more visible, we can see the force fields that create events, and we can subtly alter these with love and attention.

Then events can occur with their maximum beneficial potential, and certain dangers can be avoided or decreased. From an outer perspective this may appear magical, but it is as simple as fixing a problem in a car before it breaks down. A warning light on the dashboard or a strange noise alerts the attentive driver, and in a similar way one can be attentive to the signs of life. Watching these signs, in both the outer and the inner world, we notice when something needs our attention.

This work of watching the signs of life can be done through attention to outer events, synchronicities, as well as dreams, intuitions, subtle feelings, and experiences in meditation. These have been the tools of seers and shamans over the centuries. But we are also being given a more direct way of seeing the energy patterns of life. A new body of knowledge is being made available to us. How we approach this knowledge will determine the way it can be used and the level of the knowledge to which we are given access. If we approach it from the perspective of our individual need, we will not see the whole spectrum, and the knowledge will easily become distorted by our ego. But if our attitude is of selfless service or devotion to the divine, then different levels of knowledge will be given to us according to our need. We will be shown how to work with the energy fields of life to benefit the whole of humanity according to the need of the time and the place and the people. Because this knowledge belongs to oneness, even simple, local situations will benefit the whole.

At the highest level this knowledge will work to manifest the divine oneness more directly, more consciously, so that the meaning and joy of life will be more accessible to everyone. At lower levels we have already been given a glimpse of possible developments in technology and communication, but there will also be given

different ways of healing, and of food and energy distri-
bution, and ways of education that include the whole
human being. We will be able to move from our culture
of fragmentation and greed into a new era beyond our
present imaginings.

POWER AND MAGIC

The energy that gives sustenance to all life flows through
specific patterns, like power grids. Part of the potential
of humanity is that our consciousness can be directly
attuned to these patterns, allowing us to alter and redirect the energy that flows through them. This is a part of
our magical nature. Each human being, as a microcosm
of creation, has stamped into her consciousness the blueprint of creation, and the human brain has the potential
to access this blueprint—to directly work with the patterns of creation. There are enough connections possible in the human brain to mirror the connections of
creation, the interdependent flow of the whole of life.
The way life flows through these connections is part of
the magical knowledge of a human being.

Such knowledge has tremendous potential for power,
both positive and negative. The magus, the one who is
initiated into using this knowledge, can redirect the
energies of life for his own personal benefit. But the initiate can also work for the benefit of the whole, using
this power in service to humanity. It is a part of the law
of creation that everything in this world has a positive
and a negative side. Positive and negative forces are finely
balanced. Those who work for humanity need to consciously recognize both energies; otherwise their work
will be easily undermined. Seeing the whole means accepting the negative as well as working for the good.

Many individuals who have the spiritual potential to help humanity are unsure about stepping into the arena of this work because they know it will involve confronting the powers of darkness. There are spiritual techniques that can insulate one from these powers, allowing one to pursue one's spiritual devotions unaffected. However, these techniques also isolate the practitioner from the flow of life and prevent her from participating in the work that needs to be done.

Involvement in the world means claiming the power that is needed for the work, and this includes confronting the forces of darkness. Just as an individual has to encounter her own darkness in order to claim her real power, so too must humanity enact this confrontation on the world stage. That is one of the reasons why spiritually committed people are needed in the marketplace, in the world of commerce where so much of our contemporary power is constellated. It is here that one has direct access to the patterns of power that channel so much of the resources of our world. Only when one has access to these patterns can they be subtly altered to help bring light and laughter where at present there is only greed, desire, and deprivation.

This is not a work for the fainthearted, or for those who are frightened of making a mistake. The dangers of power are apparent, its ability to corrupt a real concern. But the adept has been trained to be always watchful, playing close attention to the warning signs that abound. And the power of love and devotion can easily untangle us from the forces that would corrupt us. It is a challenge of the present time to work with the power grid that is in the midst of the world.

When we participate in life in service to the One, the way to work with this power grid in service to oneness will make itself known. This grid is itself an expression of oneness because through it everything is connected together, in the same way that the Internet has a quality of oneness—everyone can be connected together in a global network. When enough people are consciously attuned to the power grid of creation, it will come alive with a unified consciousness that can instinctively respond to the need of the moment—energy will flow directly where it is needed. It is of great importance that as this grid becomes alive it is stamped with the name of God, so that it comes alive with the imprint of His name, with a direct, lived alignment with the Creator. Then the energy structure of the future will be alive with the consciousness of His presence and the divine will manifest into life in a new way. His oneness will become visible not only to initiates but to all those who turn towards Him.

THE SUBSTANCE OF *SIRR*

At the core of creation is an axis of light and love. Within this axis of love stand the Friends of God, merged into their Beloved, working for the world. And in their very midst stands the *qutb*, or pole of the time, the master of the Friends of God. Because they are one with God, they are also united with the whole of creation, and yet they stand separate, detached from the whirling dance of *maya*. Unattached, they are able to see where His love and power need to flow, where His majesty and beauty need to be made known. He is One and so this work is done through a state of oneness. It does not belong to the dynamics of cause and effect or past and future, but to the need of the moment. The Friends of God are present where they are needed. Working on the inner planes, they are not bound by the limitations of physical space.

And yet because they are living human beings with physical bodies, they can also embrace all the levels of creation. This enables the energy of the Beloved to come through all the levels of manifestation.

The axis of love spins at a very high frequency, and the Friends of God are dynamically attuned to this spinning. Through their spinning, a web of light and love is spun into the world. In this way, the axis of love creates a web throughout the world, throughout all the levels of creation. Through this web of light the world is sustained by a direct access to love that is not distorted by the patterns of illusion. Love is present throughout all of creation; it is the substance of every atom. Yet this substance of love does not know its own meaning or potential—it is not charged with divine consciousness. The Friends of God bring into the world a love fully charged with divine consciousness.

Love that is charged with divine consciousness has the potential to awaken humanity to its real nature and purpose. The Friends of God are here in service to this work. They have the ability to infuse a quality of divine consciousness, *sirr*, into the web of light that nourishes humanity. They can also direct this web of light where it is needed. Spiritual traditions are used to help bring this knowing into life, into the hearts of those who seek Him. This is why "transmission" or "succession" (the direct connection from teacher to teacher) is so important, as it is through this lived link that the energy of divine consciousness, *sirr*, is given. Without this link the energy of *sirr* remains on the inner planes and does not penetrate through all the levels. Then an essential part of the process is not lived; a quality of divine awareness that belongs to the physical plane does not come alive.

At each age the quality of divine knowing has a different vibration, as He reveals Himself in a new form.

New wine cannot be given in old bottles: the divine substance of *sirr* has to be given in a slightly different way in each new age. At the present time it needs to be made conscious. There needs to be a knowing of divine love. In the previous era it was given from heart to heart, from soul to soul, without conscious knowledge—it was kept secret. Even the word *sirr* means "secret." But now it needs to be made known; otherwise it cannot do its work.

The web of light, which is the highest energy pattern in the world, needs to become known. Otherwise humanity cannot take the next step in its evolution. In order for it to be made visible, a certain energy, or quality of magic, is being used. Magic is what makes the invisible world visible. The web of light that runs through the hearts of those who love Him is being charged with a quality of energy that is bringing together the inner and outer worlds, thus allowing to be known what has until now been a hidden secret.

Spiritual traditions and esoteric groups, those in service to God, have from the beginning of time been used to bring His love and wisdom into the world. As a part of this work many of these groups are allowing themselves and some of their practices to be publicly known. Many secrets are being made accessible. These different paths are also working together in a new way. This is at first happening on the inner planes, as the energies of the different paths are linking together. But this coming together is beginning to permeate consciousness, to be made known on the outer plane. The "Interfaith" movement can be seen as one aspect of this work, but there is a more powerful energy dynamic happening than just that movement.

A living spiritual tradition is a current of divine energy, and as different traditions come together on both the inner and outer planes, these currents of energy flow faster and also merge together into oneness. In oneness they do not lose their individual quality, the particular vibration or "note" that belongs to their path. Rather this note is amplified, made more perceptible and accessible. At the same time each path sings the song of divine oneness. This coming together of spiritual paths enables His hidden oneness to become more visible, and with this will come the knowledge of how oneness works in the world.

The energy of oneness is imprinted with the understanding of how oneness works. Only by recognizing the energy of oneness itself can we learn how to work with it. This is why the secret of *sirr* is being made known, because this substance of divine consciousness makes His oneness visible. Without the knowledge of *sirr* our understanding of the energy patterns of life and their purpose will remain fragmented. The heart of the world will not reveal the divine name that is at the core of humanity.

From the axis of love, from the hearts of the Friends of God, a new quality or frequency of love is being released, given to the world, to help with this work. This is a love *charged with divine consciousness*. It has already been released into the world and is beginning its work of bringing spiritual paths together and awakening a new dynamic of oneness. Love and knowledge are being brought together in a new way, so that we can have more direct access to the knowledge that we carry within our hearts and souls.

UNITING THE INNER AND OUTER

Part of the work of the lovers of God is to weave together the inner and outer worlds so that the inner can become visible, so that what is written in the book of love can become known. The worlds are being woven together with the substance of their hearts, because this is the way lovers perform their work: they give of their own essence. As the worlds are woven together, the knowledge of love and the secrets of oneness can flow more freely, unrestricted by the distinction between inner and outer.

There are forces that resist this work, that do not want such knowledge to be given freely. These forces are trying to keep the worlds apart, to stop the flow of love and knowledge. They want us to continue with our patterns of self-interest, which by their very nature keep us separate. They do not want it to be known that the secrets of life are freely available to any who look away from themselves, for then there can be no more buying and selling of spiritual commodities.

The work of bringing together the worlds has already passed the threshold: the most difficult and dangerous part of this process has been done. It cannot be reversed. The meaning of oneness is already beginning to seep through the cracks of our defenses. The work now is to make this available, to help it to flow through the web of light and love. To facilitate this work, the hearts of many different spiritual wayfarers are being linked together, because love flows fastest through the open hearts of lovers of God.

As love flows through their hearts, it brings with it the knowledge of oneness. This knowledge is imprinted into their hearts, from where it can come into consciousness. With the knowledge of oneness comes the understanding of the work that each of us needs to do, how we can best participate in this miraculous unfolding. As we participate, this knowledge is made accessible to us—the more we participate the more complete the knowledge that is given. This is a part of the way oneness works in the world. At the beginning we get just a hint, an intuition. We do not know that this hint is like a seed that contains within it a blueprint of our work. But as we live the hint, as the inner becomes part of our everyday life, the blueprint becomes gradually more accessible, its details more visible. If it is not lived the seed dries up, its potential unrealized, and the knowledge of oneness fades away.

The inner can only fully reveal its meaning when it is lived in everyday life. The outer world gives it color and substance, makes it real. And only when something becomes real can we understand its true purpose: what it means to us. The combination of the inner and the outer brings alive the secrets of life. These secrets are waiting to be lived, to come into being. But they need our full participation. Only then can they flourish, flower, and bear fruit. This is why the inner knowledge of oneness needs to be lived in the marketplace. Only then can it come alive and its wisdom and joy flower. Only then can its true potential be realized.

In previous eras the inner and outer were kept separate. The wisdom of the inner was slowly filtered to the outer. Much knowledge remained in the inner world, accessible only to initiates, those who could turn away from the outer world. Now the inner and outer need to come together: the child of the future, the consciousness of the new age, can only be born from their union. When the two worlds are kept separate, only certain energy can make the transition from the inner to the outer. When the inner and outer are united, much more energy and knowledge can flow between them. Our inner potential can become more accessible; we can live our divine nature more easily. And many different energies that can help in our evolution can flow into life. So much magic is waiting to happen. The divine has so many ways to reveal Itself, to help us know who we really are and why we are here.

THE WORLD IS WAITING

The heart of the world is awakening and beginning to sing. Its song, like all of creation, praises God, His majesty and beauty, the wonder of His world. As this song begins to be heard throughout the world, many things will come alive and flourish. The angels will hear it, and so will the hearts of human beings. This song will awaken ancient memories that have been dormant for ages. Magic will come alive, the magic that speaks to us each in our own way, calling us by our real name. Magic will also help us to see the wonder that permeates all of life. In the light of this magic we will be able to see the signs of life more clearly and understand their meaning.

The guardians of love are always with us, protecting us. At the same time we will have our own battles to fight, temptations to avoid. This world is still a shimmering of *maya*, even when it reflects His oneness more clearly. The ego will remain with its distortions, its patterns of power and dominance, its fears of vulnerability. But humanity now has the opportunity to work together, to live the natural oneness that belongs to life. Magic is now present to help this happen, to help us see how we are connected together. As different levels of reality become more visible we can see more clearly how we are linked together, how we are all part of the great river of life.

At this time of transition there are many dangers, and how we now live will affect generations to come. The magic that is being given will allow us greater access to our own personal power. And as some of the veils between the worlds fall away, we can be more easily influenced by the energies of the inner worlds, dimensions where dragons and sorcerers are real. A time of opportunity constellates darkness as well as light—it is always for us to choose.

But in the song of the world is the teaching of the present time, the way we can open to the beyond without being caught in darkness. The song of the soul of the world carries the fragrance of His love for us, a love in which everything is made sacred. This song, which we each hear in our own way, will guide us, will awaken our hearts and attune our souls. It is a most powerful magic because it reminds us who we really are, that we are the children of the orient[3] who have come from a dimension of light upon light to discover the secret of creation, the way His light is reflected in His world. The darkness is needed to make this happen, but we do not belong to the darkness.

Why do we hesitate, as if waiting for permission to step into our own future? The world is waiting for us. It needs us to acknowledge our heritage. Without our total presence and participation, the currents of love cannot flow where they are needed, memories of oneness cannot be awakened. The seeds of the future lie within our hearts but they need us to live them, and they need the darkness of the world as much as its light. We need the courage to step into the darkness that is around us, the places where power is held in the hands of greed. Those who love Him and want nothing for themselves cannot be contaminated, and they are longing to live this great adventure. They will be allowed to work with the magical powers of creation and to infuse the world with the mystical knowledge of His presence.

A NEW POWER IS PRESENT

Magic is about the immanence of the divine. Through magic we can come to experience the colors and qualities of divine presence, how He makes Himself known in His world. The world, starved of His presence, has become sick, is dying from His absence. Through the right use of magic, the world can heal itself and come alive again, alive with the knowledge of His majesty and beauty, with the wonder of every moment.

The priests of monotheism banned magic because it belongs to the manifestation of the divine, and their focus was on His transcendence. Miracles were allowed, but the conscious use of the powers of the inner world was forbidden. Our world became deprived of many of the ways to make His wonder visible *here*, to bring into the outer world the energies and qualities of the inner worlds. We became even more isolated on the physical plane of existence, lost from His presence.

Magic belongs to the feminine, to powers of manifestation, to the way life comes into the world. Magic enables many things to happen, and stops us from becoming caught in a linear and logical world. Magic turns the single light of His love into a full spectrum of color, into a wild kaleidoscope of possibilities. Magic is in the heartbeat of the world, as every moment pulses with the meeting of the known and the unknown, the visible and the invisible. Through magic the ten thousand things come alive, reflecting His oneness in a myriad of ways. Without magic life is mere existence.

We have projected our need for magic onto science and technology, and given its power to Hollywood. Magic has become an industry rather than a celebration. Often we are manipulated rather than brought alive. Instead of giving us a taste of the secrets of creation, a glimpse of the beauty of revelation, it presents us with yet another veil of illusion. We have created an idea of magic that imprisons us in our fantasies rather than opening our eyes to His unending mystery. Real magic always points us to what is hidden, to His indefinable nature.

Science has opened our eyes to many of His mysteries. But as a masculine, analytic discipline, it is often blind to the play of relationships, to the symphony of interconnections that are always present. And it has focused our attention on the physical world, limiting our access to the invisible realms. Masculine and feminine, the outer and the inner, need to be brought together. We need to embrace the unknown rather than try to control it.

Mystics and lovers of God have always known about powers beyond the physical world. They have had their hearts burned by an unseen fire, their world turned upside down again and again. They have been seduced and tricked by an unknowable Beloved, made fools by their loving. Their inner eye has seen dimensions of light and a dazzling darkness. In the midst of the world they live in both the visible and the invisible, and they bring the sweet fragrance of the beyond into daily life. They hold the keys to the inner worlds and know the mysteries written in humanity's heart.

And now there is a new power being made available, more potent than before. It can open the inner doors of darkness and light and make visible the real colors of creation. Those who love Him are being given access to this power, and are being asked to use it for His sake. It has the potential to redeem the whole world, to clear away the debris and pollution that cover its beauty. The heart of the world has awakened and is asking for our help, not just on the inner planes but in the midst of life. When we give ourself to life for His sake, for the sake of His love for us, this power will be present and will begin to work its magic.

Imagination

The Human Imagination: throwing off the temporal that the eternal might be established.

William Blake[1]

PARTICIPATING IN THE ARCHETYPAL REALM

The imagination is a powerful means of accessing and working with the inner world. Through the faculty of the imagination one can move from the world of the senses to an interior dimension, the symbolic realm of the soul. But we have forgotten this higher potential of the imagination because our culture focuses so completely on the world of the senses and the abstract realm of thought.

Working with the inner world requires us to restore the higher purpose of the imagination and understand how it functions. First, though, it is necessary to accept that there are different levels of reality, which have different properties. We are surrounded by the physical world of the senses, and yet through our dreams we have an open doorway to the realm of the soul, which is a world of archetypal images. Traditionally, symbolic art has also been a vehicle to express the beauty and terror of this world of the gods, though in recent years art has been more often used to explore the world of the personal unconscious, which lacks the eternal quality of the soul.

The archetypal realm of the soul is not the only interior dimension. There are many different levels of reality, which can be accessed by different faculties. The inner plane of the Self (known in Sanskrit as the *atmic* plane) is initially revealed through grace. Later it can be accessed by pure love or pure consciousness, *Bodhi.* In this realm the pure essence of all things exists undistort- ed. It is a realm of *light upon light,* in which the light of the Creator and the created are merged together. Expe- riencing this level of reality, we discover our own essen- tial nature, "the face we had before we were born."

Beyond the realm of the Self there are planes of non- being, the dazzling darkness, which contain the secrets of our nonexistence. On the Sufi path these planes of non-being are reached through merging with the *sheikh,* who is merged with God. The *sheikh* is one who has been made empty, whose inner essence has been dissolved— he spins in the vortex of nothingness. The realm of the Self, which is pure being, and the further dimensions of non-being cannot be accessed through the imagination.

The archetypal world, or world of the gods, is the intermediate dimension between the physical world of the senses and the plane of the Self. Carl Jung stresses the importance of this world of images, describing the archetypal realm and its collective psychology as "the powerful factor, the factor which changes our whole life, which changes the surface of our known world, which makes history."[2] When we enter this realm we step away from the controlled and predictable world of our senses and begin familiarizing ourself with the unknown, the unpredictable. In the archetypal world we open ourselves to richer experiences and deeper meaning, gain a greater understanding of who we are and the world we live in. The archetypal world also prepares us and helps us to access the luminous dimension of the Self.

Jung understood how the imagination functions as a means of experiencing the inner symbolic world. He also developed a technique of "active imagination" to explore it consciously. In contrast to the dream state where the symbolic is experienced solely at the unconscious level, in "active imagination" the individual *consciously* encounters the imaginal, and is able to *consciously* participate with the figures that inhabit the archetypal world.

Jung developed "active imagination" from his own personal encounters with the collective unconscious, but he subsequently grounded this technique in his discovery of the use of the imagination in alchemy. The alchemists made the important distinction between *Imaginatio* and *Phantasia*. In *Imaginatio* the individual consciously participates in the imaginative process, while *Phantasia* is merely the spinning of aimless or groundless fantasies. Alchemists used *Imaginatio* in the work of transformation, as a means for guiding an individual beyond his limitations and expanding his horizons of being.

Fantasy or daydreaming is a passive process, like watching pictures on a screen. In contrast, an encounter with the archetypal world demands that an individual consciously take part in the inner drama, which must be a fully-felt experience. Jung uses Parsifal as an example. As a mere lad, Parsifal found the grail king, but "forgot to ask the vital question because he was not aware of his participation in the event." The grail castle vanished, and Parsifal did not find the grail until he returned many years later.

Henry Corbin, an Islamist and a follower of Jung, recognized a similar use of imagination in the Sufism of Ibn 'Arabî. Ibn 'Arabî saw the world of the imagination as a bridge or "intermediary between the world of Mystery ('âlam al-ghayb) and the world of visibility ('âlam al-shahâdat)."[3] Through the imagination we have access to an intermediary, symbolic world, which Corbin describes as the *mundus imaginalis*, whose images correspond to "a fundamental psychic structure."[4] The use of the imagination in this tradition causes the symbolic essence of a material form, as it exists in the world of Mystery, to be perceived, uniting the inner and outer worlds. Corbin stressed that the imaginal world is an objective reality. Like Jung, he understood the possibility of collective understanding, of common perception, in this unfamiliar realm.

There is also a dimension of this symbolic realm where specific energies or images have yet to form. This dimension is comprised of archetypal energies prior to personification, before they become imaged as gods, goddesses, or other figures. Here, these energies exist as fluid patterns with specific qualities.

In our physical world we are used to differentiation by separation. In the archetypal world "one thing is never one thing" and the lines of differentiation are less clear. Our dreams and our creativity portray this more fluid, amorphous reality, in which images change, shift, and evolve. Even the concept of different realms of existence suggests a linear, hierarchical image, while all these different levels interpenetrate, are all expressions of the same primal oneness. The closer one comes to the dimension of the Self the more fully this oneness is visible.

HEALING THE ARCHETYPAL WORLD

The use of the imagination to access and work with the inner world has also been the domain of the shaman. Shamans are taught how to enter the inner world, often going on a shamanic journey where they encounter power animals and other spirit helpers. They heal by helping others find their own power animal or spirit guides that reconnect them to the energies of the archetypal realm. Power animals and other shamanic beings are living images through which the meaning and energy of the archetypal world are made accessible. These beings are transformers of psychic energy, allowing us access to the energies of the inner world while protecting us from their primal, undifferentiated power. They have a function similar to the symbols of a religion, as in the example of the wine and chalice of the Catholic Church, through which the blood of Christ can nourish the ordinary person.

The shaman is always in service to the tribe, to the well-being of others, and also to the gods themselves. In order to work in these realms we must follow their example. If we approach these archetypal energies from the perspective of our individual well-being, we will see only a small fragment of the whole, and our imaginative capacity will remain imprisoned. If we can turn our attention away from the individual self, our imagination will open its doors and we will begin to see the whole spectrum: the psychic structure of life. And through the correct use of the imagination we can learn to work with these archetypal energies, to reconnect our whole culture with its primal power. Then real healing can begin.

Through our active imaginal participation we can learn about the inhabitants of the archetypal realm, their sorrows and joys, their potential and problems. Only too often we discover that they have been waiting to speak with us, to share their wisdom and power. Unable to directly cross into our world, they need us to come to them, to consciously communicate with them. Then they welcome us as brothers and sisters, lovers or friends. They need us to understand the problems that our neglect has caused, how we have desecrated the temples of the inner world and harmed its inhabitants.

Many new spiritual teachings are showing us how archetypal figures can help us reconnect with the forgotten inner world and with the gods and goddesses who abide there, in order to empower ourselves, heal our addictions, and bring a sacred dimension to our lives. But we have been blind to how the archetypes need us. For hundreds of years our culture has decreed that the archetypal world does not exist, and such rejection has caused much pain to the archetypes. In particular the archetypal feminine has been deeply wounded, and often appears as a woman blinded by her tears and grief. The archetypal world needs our help. It is waiting to be transformed. Sunlight and laughter need to return to this symbolic world. And it needs the participation of individual consciousness to make this happen. We can bring the seed of joy to this land we have made barren.

Through our conscious participation in the inner world, the temples of the imagination can be rebuilt, the sacred nature of our soul reestablished. The archetypal figures can show us what to do. Like planets circling in their fixed orbits, these primal powers cannot move freely in their inner word, they cannot connect with their own source of healing. They need us, for if our motives are pure we can travel freely in the imaginal world. We can find a mother's lost child, or a healing herb for a poisoned knight. If we approach them with respect, they will give us the wisdom and understanding we need for this work. They will show us how to travel in their world, give us a magical sword for power and discrimination, an invisible cloak for protection, a crystal sphere of light for wisdom.

WORKING WITH THE INNER WORLD

Working with the energy patterns of life is just a different perspective to working with archetypal figures. Seen from the perspective of the personal psyche, these archetypal energies are personified. But seen from a more impersonal perspective, these energies can take the form of dynamic patterns. Working with these energy patterns requires that we first recognize that they exist, and then look for them with our imagination. Once we turn our attention towards the inner world, the living energy of that realm will take form to meet us. The forms might differ from person to person, depending on the qualities of the person or the need of the moment. Often they appear dimly at first, emerging and dissolving. Just as the grail castle is often hidden by swirling mist or fog, the inner world comes to us veiled by our rational self. Then, as our attention is drawn to it, the dancing structure of life becomes more visible, more distinct.

Holding these patterns in our imagination, we begin to dialogue with them. They are dynamically alive and respond to our conscious attention. Through this interaction they reveal their meaning, their needs, and the ways we can serve them. This knowledge is imprinted into the energy structure itself, but is only made visible through our individual participation.

The archetypal world is only accessible through the individual—we can only directly experience it within ourself. And because the archetypal dimension helps to express and manifest our own unique individual nature, for each of us the meaning and nature of our participation will be slightly different.

Through the power of the imagination, we can work with the energy structures of life and help redeem an imbalance that has built up over centuries. Our consciousness has the potential to unblock or, if necessary, redirect energy, and the more we work with the inner world, the more we become attuned to its needs. Just as a healer becomes sensitive to the signs and energy patterns of the body, so can we become attentive to the subtle needs of life's inner core. Watching the currents of life, the pulse of creation, we feel where we are needed, where we are called to participate. Often a quality of attention is required, sometimes focused, sometimes more diffuse. Or we are asked to bring love to a certain place. Sometimes just following the course of a flow of energy is all that is needed; or we have to make a connection between threads of energy, holding this connection in our imagination until the work is done. Some threads need to be woven together, making a new pattern.

Patterns of energy have different forms. Some are like Celtic knots, flowing back upon themselves, while others are more like strands that are kept separate. There are also places of power from which many lines radiate, while in other areas the lines of power are few and far between, their light diffuse. And there are places of chaos where no pattern seems visible. Sometimes this chaos is more dynamic than any order, while sometimes it is like a knot of energy which needs to be untangled. Some energy patterns pulse and move, while others seem more tranquil, like a deep, slow-moving river. And always we are guided to where we are needed, to where our attention is required.

As we work with the inner world, it responds; a dialogue develops. The connections and patterns in our mind can become synchronized with life's energy patterns, and they can talk to each other, brought together by our consciousness. Slowly we realize that we are holding the archetypal world in our mind, that we are a part of the same dynamic oneness. This is when the real magical work is done, as the interconnections in our own consciousness mirror those of both the inner and outer worlds. We are a part of life as it comes into being, contributing our gift of consciousness to the evolution of the whole.

THE BOOK OF LIFE

Archetypal images or patterns are a blueprint of humanity, through which flow the energies of life that give us purpose and meaning. As we consciously work with the inner world, individual and collective consciousness dance together. The archetypes, the impersonal forces that shape our destiny, welcome and embrace our individual self. They become our partner in the flow of life, and from this union a new quality of consciousness is born: the child of the future who knows what is written in the book of life.

Knowing what is written in the book of life allows us to work directly with our own destiny as it is written, not through the mirrors of distortion. We waste so much energy in unnecessary endeavors, attempting things that are not meant to happen. If we can work directly with our own destiny, our evolution will speed up. We will be able to focus our attention and resources where they are needed, where they can achieve real results. When our outer life reflects more visibly the imprint of our destiny, the outer world will cease to be a mirror of illusion. Instead life will point more directly to our essence, and even the most mundane experiences will carry an imprint of divine meaning and divine presence.

Following the thread of our destiny, how it is woven into the events of our life, we can catch the meaning of our soul. The soul lives itself through the pattern of our destiny, through the colors of the day and its web of light and darkness. In our destiny the soul reveals itself, not as a hidden mystery but in the substance of life. And so the meaning of matter, of the soul coming into incarnation, is made known.

As the soul's purpose becomes more visible, its music can be heard. And in the music of our soul is the music of the whole world, for we are a part of this whole. Our individual destiny is a part of the destiny of the world. In our ordinary life the deepest meaning of the world can be read; its destiny is written in the book of our life.

Living our destiny brings together the two worlds, the inner and outer, what is hidden and what is revealed. Our destiny is the golden thread that holds together the hearts of humanity and the heart of the world. We carry the heart of the world within our own heart, and through living our destiny we nourish the heart of the world. We speak to the soul of the world in the language of life, a life that carries the imprint of the divine names, of His purpose. Living our destiny, we write the names of God in the book of life. This is part of the purpose of humanity, and when we live this purpose, life is awakened to His beauty and His majesty.

Through living our destiny we bring the primal power of oneness into being, because His oneness is stamped into the core of our soul. The power of His oneness is needed in the world: it can heal the divisions and distortions that scatter us, that make us fight each other and ourselves. Through oneness many things can be revealed, many things can happen. Life is waiting for the imprint of the soul of each of us to release the energy of oneness.

THE *CONIUNCTIO*

Western thought locates the realm of the soul within a hierarchical structure of existence, a metaphor originating in Plato. The lowest of the levels of existence is the sensory world, from which one can ascend to the ideal world of "Ideas" and "Forms." The intermediate position of the soul, between the sensory world and the world of "Forms," gives it the potential to link the different levels and see the unity within the multiplicity of sense impressions. Plotinus, developing Platonic theory, also saw the soul as occupying an intermediate rank, "what comes after it is this world and what is before is the contemplation of real being."[5] Moreover Plotinus linked the soul with the imagination. He saw that the sensible world is translated into the images of the soul by the soul's imaginative faculty.[6]

Platonic theory had a deep impact on Western thought, and also on Islamic mysticism. Ibn 'Arabî and the eleventh-century physician-philosopher-mystic Avicenna recognized the imagination as a vehicle for visionary ascent to a higher level of reality. If we are to reclaim the use of the imagination, we need to embrace its soul quality and yet move beyond a hierarchical model and its image of ascent. In the circle of oneness everything is present. There is no above and below, no ascending or descending. These are images of the past millennium. All the levels of reality interpenetrate, and the "highest" is present within each of us. The soul pervades the body from head to toe. Every cell is impregnated with His essence. And between the particles of creation is the infinite emptiness that carries the secrets of non-being.

The potential of the imagination is to bring together levels of reality that we had perceived as separate, to unite the inner and outer so that we can live in both worlds with open eyes. We can no longer afford to keep the worlds separate, because the outer world needs the nourishment that can only come from within. The imagination can nourish us with meaning from the inner world, with its beauty and power. And when the two worlds begin to flow together, when the inner and outer unite within our consciousness and our lives, something new can come alive. This is the child of the future, born from the *coniunctio*, that carries the secret of the New Age. She is both male and female, outer and inner, above and below, spirit and matter. She is within each of us and yet beyond us. She knows the secrets of matter and the majesty of *light upon light.*

When the child of the future awakens, we will come to see ourself in a new way. We will know why we are here more clearly and completely. She will create a new civilization and give us the tools we need to take us into the future. We will regain our magical nature, our knowing of how the outer and inner worlds work together. She will tell each of us our own story, our own myth of becoming. A veil that has hidden us from ourself will be removed, gradually and gently. And when this veil has been removed we will be able to see the dawn that has already arrived. Then we will be able to walk in the sunshine of our real Self. The beauty and sorrow of this world of *maya* will remain, but we will see its meaning and purpose with greater clarity.

Then the force fields of life will change; the patterns of creation will open in a new way. At the moment these patterns are tightly constricted. This is partly what keeps our attention focused on the physical plane. When they open we will see what is behind them, what at the moment appears like empty space. So many levels of reality are hidden from us: we see only the leaves of the great tree of life.

The child of the future is waiting to come alive, a promise that needs to be lived. She will show us how we are a part of life, not as survivors, but as celebrants. We are a part of a tremendous intimacy we call creation, a beautiful, violent, erotic explosion made of stardust and love. Our motion is bonded to the motion of the moon and the sun, of the galaxy, of a spider spinning its web in the corner of a room or between blades of grass.

When the inner and outer worlds start to dance together, the patterns of creation will change. They will come alive with the consciousness of humanity in a new way. They will respond to our vision: help us to recreate the world. If we let them, they can help us redeem the damage that we have done, cleanse the waters of toxins and our thought-forms of greed. Then, when the natural balance of creation has been restored, the civilization of the next age can emerge.

RECLAIMING THE IMAGINATION

One of the tools we have been given to help in this work is the correct use of the imagination. We have been conditioned to think that the imagination belongs only to the inner world, which is why it has been disregarded as daydreams or fantasies. But once the inner and outer are linked together, the imagination will work with archetypal forms and energy lines so that they can benefit life as a whole. When we begin this work, ancient memories will surface, memories that we carry in our ancestral self, of how this work is done. We already have the knowledge we need. Like the language of dreams, it is within us, even if almost forgotten. Reclaiming this knowledge, this ancient way of knowing, is one of the first steps that we need to take.

How do we reclaim the correct use of the imagination? In the same way that we learn the language of our dreams. We watch and listen with attention. The signs are all around us. The dawn has already arrived. The unicorns that have before never left the forest are present in our city streets. They are glowing with light. They have children riding on their backs who belong with them. Why are they unnoticed? We have forgotten to look, but also we think that they are elsewhere. We never imagine that they could be with us, here at the street corner.

The dust has been swept from the doorway which has been engraved with the symbols of the future. That work has already been done. Our work is to read the symbols, to unfold our own future. We have been given permission to work with the energy lines of life. When we begin this work we recognize our place as the doorway between the worlds. We are the magic that is waiting to happen. We are the song of God.

The Children of the Orient

There is something more important than being wise,
and that is to love freely and unendingly, letting
everything grow and flow in its own nature, not trying
to impose our nature, but by being alive oneself in
such a way as to bring others alive too.

Cecil Collins[1]

THE FLOW OF LIFE

Life's natural simplicity has been forgotten. This is not
the apparent simplicity of bygone eras, when our outer
life was less complex. It is the simplicity of relating to life
as a continual flow rather than relating to a multitude of
events that fill our days or years. Contemporary culture
confronts us with life as a plurality of different events,
each one demanding our attention to a greater or lesser
degree. And as our culture seems to speed up, so these
events appear to multiply, and our attention span de-
creases as we inevitably fail to keep up with everything
that happens around us. It is as if we are flowing faster
and faster down the river of life, and as our attention
remains focused on the river banks, we see objects,
people, situations move past more and more quickly.

We cannot stop the river, just as we cannot slow
down the evolution of our culture. But we can learn to
look at life in a different way. If we see life just from the
perspective of the objects on the banks, our life will
become an indistinguishable blur as we try to assimilate

everything that is passing us by. But if our attention shifts to the flow of the river, to the water that carries us, then a fundamental simplicity will return. We will no longer be trying to catch up on what is passing by, but will realize that we are part of the natural process of life itself that is always changing and yet retains its essential qualities.

Looking to the banks of the river, we see the isolated incidents of life, the seemingly static objects that pass us by. The faster the flow, the more these seem to change, and the more anxious and insecure we become as we try to hold on to what is passing. Although we are caught in a flow we cannot stop, or even slow down, we try to give ourself an image of stability by keeping our attention on the fixed objects on the river banks. But maybe life is trying to turn our attention elsewhere, to have us realize a different attitude, one that does not define life by distinct objects or fixed events, but by movement itself, by the very dynamic of change.

Earlier cultures saw life in terms of the changing seasons, a natural turning of which they were a part. In this continual change everything had its place; even times of drought or hardship were valued. But as we imposed ourself upon nature, so we separated ourself from life's flow and saw life in terms of what we could possess. We have now increased our possessions so that they fill not only our garages but our imaginations, and we have created a culture of consumerism to indulge our desires. And yet we do not realize how this attitude has isolated us, capturing our attention with the fixed objects of our desires and so separating us from the flow and movement of life itself.

Life is a dynamic process of continual change, and we live at a time in which this change is more and more visible. It is no longer a gentle succession of the seasons, but a time in which not only technology but even the climate patterns are changing beyond our expectations. And these changes are no longer local, but global. We are being asked to see our individual life in a new way, and yet in the West where these changes are most apparent, they are producing stress rather than joy. Are we just the victims of our own technological success, which has created a monster we can no longer control? Or is it that we are just looking at life in the wrong way, unable or unwilling to make the shift that will reveal what life is offering us? Perhaps making this shift is as easy as attuning ourselves differently, to the flow of life rather than to fixed objects of our desire.

But do we have the courage to make this shift when so much of our identity lies in what we possess? To become attuned to the flow of life means to recognize that things are both lost and found. We have the opportunity and responsibility to see life as it is presenting itself to us now—not as an accumulation of desires or goals, but as movement and change. We can regain the simple wonder of life if we relate to life as a flow of events, as a pattern of continually changing interrelationships. The multiplicity of life will no longer bombard us as a confusing discord of events, but reveal its deeper purpose, the patterns it is trying to make visible. Life then becomes our partner in the great destiny of uncovering our own soul.

THE WHOLENESS OF LIFE

Life is present all around us and we are a part of life. If we stand outside of life, the ten thousand things bombard us relentlessly, and we are pushed further and further to the abyss of confusion and despair. But if we stand within the circle of life, then all of its multiplicity is a natural out-pouring of life's abundance, nourishing and supporting us, and helping us to realize our true self. The deepest purpose of life is to reflect what is hidden, to reveal the unknowable essence of which we are all an expression. Separate from life, we confront only our own separate-ness, our isolation and suffering. Simply to recognize that we are a part of life is to radically alter our percep-tion of ourself and our surroundings. We are then able to perceive the patterns of which we are a part, the mani-festation of the divine which is our true nature.

We are so caught in the complexities of our culture that we do not realize how a simple shift in attitude can have such a radical and transformational effect. We have forgotten how life reveals itself: that it is not a puzzle to be solved or a conflict to be resolved, but a mystery that unveils itself. The complex interrelationships of life are real, but they are part of a greater wholeness, a wholeness that is present in every cell of creation. Only if we are able to perceive life from the perspective of wholeness will we be able to recognize the work that needs to be done.

The wholeness of life is both around us and within us, and yet we do not know how to see it. We see only the isolated events of our own life, rather than the currents that form them. We do not know how to watch the cur-rents of life: how they create and destroy, and how we are a part of this unfolding pattern. We see only the events after they have constellated: only then do we recognize the patterns that have created them. We do not know how life constellates around us, and how we influence and affect this dynamic. The simple wisdom of watching the flow of life is as foreign to us as a hieroglyphic script carved on ancient temple walls. And yet our life has become too complex to be understood without reference to the patterns that create it. We will never resolve the global problems that continually confront us unless we access humanity's inherent ability to interact with and influence the flow of events, the patterns of creation as they come into being.

Life has always presented humanity with new challenges to help us evolve and grow. Yet at each stage we are reluctant to "take upon us the mystery of things," but would rather remain with tools and attitudes that belong to a previous era. But a new way of life is waiting to come into being, and it needs us as midwives. We do not have to perform heroic feats or learn complex tasks. We just need to recognize the simple wonder of being alive, of being a part of life. A fundamental shift in attitude is all that is required; an ability to recognize what is most apparent, that we are a part of life, life that is whole and complete despite its obvious distortions, its discord of light and dark, suffering and happiness.

Caught between the opposites, we endlessly battle our shadow. But there is something greater that needs to be lived, a oneness that contains the opposites, a wholeness in which all is included. Watching the flow of life, we can see these opposites, how each has its part to play. And yet there is also a way to avoid unnecessary suffering, to step outside the cycle of self-destruction both in our own life and collectively. Whether we can make this step depends upon those who can see beyond their ego-self and be in service to the greater whole. Then life will open its doors of meaning and help us to redeem what we have almost destroyed. We will be shown how to help the energies of life flow freely on all levels. This knowledge is waiting to be given to humanity.

THE POTENCY OF DARKNESS

Hidden within life is the key to this knowledge. It is no longer to be found in esoteric books or ancient rituals. It is present all around us. But we have been conditioned to look elsewhere, and so we cannot see what is here. We have forgotten how to see life as a place of revelation. Instead we see our surroundings through the veils of our desires, and are always searching for what we do not have. We believe in the propaganda of dissatisfaction, while our workdays are distorted by the goals we are asked to achieve. The mystery of life is here, in every moment, given freely, waiting to be received.

How can it be so simple? We should ask instead, why should it not be simple? Why should what we are being given be complex or difficult? Why should we have to pay for what belongs to us, what is our own birthright? In the circle of His oneness everything is always present, complete. Only our eyes of distortion cannot see it. Seeing through the mind's patterns of complexity, we see complexity around us. Seeing with the sincerity of the heart, we glimpse the oneness of all life and its divine simplicity. God is a simple essence, far beyond our understanding and yet stamped in every cell of our being.

Every moment is dynamically alive with His presence. His presence is not an isolated occurrence, not a single sighting to be revered and remembered, but an outpouring of love that is a constant stream of the divine coming into being. It cannot be captured, held as an icon. It needs to be lived. We are a part of the living substance of God that is in constant motion as It reveals Itself again and again, "never in the same form twice." Each moment is complete, and each moment is a part of life's continual outpouring. If we see only the isolated moments, we lose the magic, the wonder, the joy. Focusing on what seems fixed and unchanging, we are blind to what life has to offer us.

Yet we long to hold life static and so save ourselves from the darkness and chaos that are around us. We have built so many walls and concepts to protect ourselves from life's unending metamorphosis. We even try to remain young, to keep our bodies in some idealized image of youth or beauty. Our goals and ideals offer a crystallized view of the future, frozen into an image for which we work and aspire. And so we deny the very reality of life, which becomes a monster from which we try to escape. Are we so frightened of what life has to offer us that we need to deny its essential nature of change?

If life does not change, it dies, and yet paradoxically we are so frightened of death that we try to hold back the flow of life. Without knowing it, we are caught in a masculine idealized image, a longing for perfection that denies the feminine with its understanding of darkness, decay, and destruction. Without darkness there can be no birth; nothing creative can take place. Without destruction there can be no cycle of life, only a sterile environment in which nothing grows. If we do not accept the darkness, life will lose whatever meaning it has left. If we do not allow ourself to live in the darkness, the doors of revelation will remain closed.

Initiates have always known that rebirth only happens in the darkness. In the moist darkness of the feminine, new life is conceived and carried. Should our culture be different, reborn only in the light, in the brightness of consciousness? When we envisage a future of technological or scientific progress, we avoid the darkness, just as we have turned away from the primal power of the feminine that is the real giver of life. And so the sterility of our disbelief surrounds us, because we do not dare to welcome the darkness, the unknowing, the wisdom of the feminine.

Life demands darkness: just as the river surface sparkles in the sunlight, so does it have its depths. In the depths there is silence, there is a slow-moving balance to the myriad reflections of the surface. The depths carry a quality of life that is essential, even if it is unknowable. We cannot afford to live much longer only on the surface of life. The real promise of our future demands that we accept the darkness of our own destruction and greed, and discover within this darkness the seeds of our own unhappiness: how we have denied ourself something essential to life.

Yet our fast-moving culture seems to have little time for introspection or descent. We are continually bombarded by demands, by the problems or achievements that require our immediate attention. The darkness is an outsider, unwanted, rejected. We see only the destructive powers of darkness, the way it can disturb our ambitions, deny us what we want. The darkness holds a gun or knife to rob us of our possessions. Its potential for rebirth, for resurrection, for revelation, has been long purged from our collective thought-forms. When the priests came with their soldiers and swords to destroy the temples of priestesses and cut down their sacred groves, the potency of darkness was trampled underfoot. For a while this wisdom was carried by the Gnostics and alchemists, but the religious hierarchies of masculine power were threatened by something they could not control, and persecution followed. Yet the flow of life needs darkness, needs the depths; and the feminine carries the instinctual wisdom of what is. She knows the simplicity of life, how it comes into being and is always a mystery and wonder. She holds this knowledge in her body, in her very nature.

THE FEMININE CARRIES THE CONNECTIONS OF LIFE

In the bright light of masculine consciousness, each object stands out clear and distinct. In the diffuse consciousness of the feminine, the patterns of relationship are more visible. The feminine carries the connections of all of life within her, and for many centuries this has been her secret. Even when the masculine degraded and punished her, abused and rejected her instinctual understanding, she still carried this wisdom, even as it became hidden from her own conscious knowing. Now this wisdom is needed. It can no longer be hidden, but needs to become conscious.

The connections of life are all around us. But while men may know this in abstract, women carry this understanding in the cells of their body. They feel the pulse of life in a way that is inaccessible to men. The cells of a woman's body carry a light that is not present in a man's body. This is because she is a part of the sacred mystery of creation. She is always a part of the whole of life. Her knowing is not abstract but lived.

The connections of life carry the seeds of the future, of what is being given to humanity. It is through these connections that the energy of life flows. Our understanding of the energy flow of life depends upon our knowledge of the interconnectedness of all of life and how these connections are made. We also need to know how connections can become damaged, torn, destroyed, and how to repair, to mend what has been broken. We need to regain the knowledge of how the threads of life are woven, how the tapestry of creation is formed. We need to bring this feminine wisdom into consciousness so that we can learn to relate to the whole of life.

We can only work with the flow of life when we understand the connections through which life flows.

We need to regain an understanding of the dynamics of the relationships that bind together all of creation. The feminine holds this natural knowing within her. It is a part of her instinctual connection to life: she contains within her body the sacred essence of creation. But to protect this sacred knowing from the ravages of the patriarchy and its misuse of power, she hid her wisdom. It was never written down in books, but transmitted from mother to daughter, from priestess to initiate. Then, when the wise women were persecuted and burned, when it became no longer safe to have any access to this knowing, it was pushed into the unconscious.

Many times in the course of humanity, esoteric wisdom has been hidden and so protected from misuse. Sometimes this wisdom can never be regained: for example, many of the secrets of sacred geometry have been lost forever. But if there is a real need, then the wisdom can be recovered. Certain sacrifices have to be made, however. The women who hold this knowledge are still fearful of the power of the patriarchy and its potential for misuse. They carry in their ancient memories the scars of persecution, and often a deep anger towards the masculine. But they have to put aside their own misgivings, and bring their inner knowing into the light of consciousness. Certain connections need to be made within the foreseeable future. If these connections are not made, then humanity will move into the dark ages that so often follow the end of a civilization.

If the connections of life are made known, then light can travel through these connections, awakening centers of consciousness within humanity. The light of masculine consciousness cannot find these centers without the full participation of the feminine. The connections cannot be made that will awaken them. Without the activation of these centers of consciousness, humanity cannot take the next step in its spiritual evolution. It will not have access to the wisdom, power, and love that it needs. Humanity will then remain fragmented, rather than learning to function as a dynamic, interrelated whole. Patterns of energy-flow around the planet will remain dormant, or function on a lower level. Once again humanity will have missed an opportunity.

Of course there is always the danger that the wisdom of the feminine will be misused. The hierarchies of power can use the knowledge of life's connections for their own personal ambition and greed. But those who look after the destiny of our planet have balanced the forces of light and dark so as to give humanity the optimum opportunity to make this step. Humanity now needs to take responsibility for its own future. A certain work has been done, however, to create the best circumstances for this transition. The danger is real but has been allowed for. The women who have access to the wisdom of life must make their own personal choice: whether to face the possible danger and the real pain of the past and bring their inner knowing into the outer world.

Certain women have already made this step, and a certain knowledge has been given back to humanity. But the next step is the most difficult, because this involves the knowledge that is held within the physical body of women. Women have been physically abused for so many centuries that this knowledge is covered in pain and anger. To bring this knowledge into the open would require a degree of vulnerability that is frightening. Yet it is necessary. Without the full participation of the feminine, the energy of oneness cannot become part of the earth. The physical body of the feminine is the connection between heaven and earth. Without this connection a quality of joy and belonging to God cannot be lived; oneness will not be made manifest.

It is for each woman to make the choice for herself. This is the nature of free will. There are many valid reasons why she should not share her knowledge, and yet there is a need that is pressing. This step can only be made by women because they have suffered the abuse and persecution in their own bodies. This is one of the laws of destiny. Women have the freedom to deny us all the future.

But women more than men also know of the sanctification that comes through suffering. They experience this with the pain and joy of childbearing, with the wonder of giving new life. Suffering belongs to the mystery of life, and, as in the image of Christ on the cross, suffering also belongs to rebirth. Suffering can make sacred, can reconnect the temporal and the divine. This is one of the esoteric meanings of the crucifixion, the cross of suffering in which the horizontal and vertical meet. Our nature, both human and divine, makes us suffer in a way that does not belong to the animal kingdom. We can suffer consciously, and we can consecrate our suffering by consciously offering it to our Creator. This is one of the paths of redemption that bring together our temporal and spiritual self.

Through suffering life can be made holy. A woman knows this in her body. Through suffering the immortal spirit takes on form, the soul comes into manifestation. This is not self-inflicted or self-indulgent suffering, not the suffering behind which we hide, that protects us from life or ourself. This is the suffering that life brings us naturally, that is part of the destiny of the soul. Suffering can transform us and help us remember who we are. It can lift the coverings of the soul. In the words of Keats, this world of tears is also "the vale of Soulmaking."

THE SUFFERING OF THE EARTH

Women carry in their body not only the consciousness of their own suffering, but also the suffering of the earth. Women carry the imprint of all of creation within their body; it is a part of their instinctual relationship to the whole of life, the sacred bond that women have with life. The suffering of the earth, wounded and desecrated by a patriarchal culture that sees God only in heaven, is held within the cellular structure of every woman. The pain that many women feel in the core of their being is also the unacknowledged pain of the earth, whose very eco-system is now in danger. This suffering needs to be accepted and sanctified; otherwise the energy of life cannot flow freely within the earth.

The earth has cried and women have felt its tears. In these tears a deep sorrow and wounding are acknowledged and through the heart offered to Him who is source of all sorrow and all joy. On our individual journey, sorrow takes us deeper within ourself, for "God enters through a wound." Through the world's sorrow a healing can take place in which the consciousness of divine love can be infused into the hidden places of the earth, as well as the bodies of women. This love can link the two worlds in a way that has not happened before. Through it His grace can flow freely, bringing alive the meaning and magic that lie at the core of creation, the secret of the word *Kun!* (Be).

If women are prepared to recognize the sacred dimension of their own and the earth's suffering at the hands of the patriarchy, to see that it is part of the mysterious destiny of the soul of our world, then much can be redeemed. We can step from the arena of personal antagonism into the landscape of our larger destiny, and the forces of life can flow in a new way. The divine can become conscious more completely, the oneness become known more fully. The soul of the world is crying to be heard, and only those who have suffered can fully recognize her. Behind the veil of her tears she has a new face, and in her eyes the stars are again visible. But we cannot wait too long in the antechamber of the heart. The soul of the world needs to know that she has been heard, so that her tears can be washed away by the waters of life. Then once again life can become sacred. Only then can the joy of life return to each moment. Only then can the imprint of His face become visible, the glory of His oneness be made known.

SHADOWS OF THE PAST

And yet we wait. Always we wait, as if reluctant to take a step into the unknown. We look around for comfort and security, even spiritual security. We want to be sure that we are doing the right thing. But there is no "right thing." The feminine knows that the darkness is real and life-giving. The feminine also knows the secrets of love and longing, because love is a feminine mystery. Yet she is reluctant to live her real passion, just as the masculine is reluctant to leave the safety of what he knows, the positions of power he has established over centuries. Then what is waiting for us will never be lived.

Each time when humanity has come to this step it has turned back. Can this moment be different? Can we walk forward together, men and women, naked, unafraid of either the light or the darkness?

In a dream a window is open, and a dove is flying towards the window, carrying a letter at her feet. In fact she is flying upon this letter. The letter is written by two children of the orient who want their parents to come together again, one living in the orient and one living in the occident. This letter has such a deep call, such longing in it. And the two children are not only about the coming together of east and west, of feminine and masculine, but about a new link between future and past, and between the unknown and the known.

To live this dream takes courage and foolishness. We are restless and uncertain, as we should be at the beginning of such a venture. But something needs to be lived, completely, without excuses. Only then can we be given what is waiting for us. The masculine and feminine need to come together in a new way, so that the feminine can step into the light and the masculine give up his position of dominance. These opposites have constellated so much antagonism, but that can be left behind, just as a ship leaves behind the shore. It has become too dangerous to remain under the influence of our convictions: too much power has been constellated to be resolved through mediation. Life and love can guide us, the flow of the current can take us. Certain currents have come near to the shore that were not here before. They are here for our journey. The beyond is beckoning us, and it has sent its emissaries of both light and darkness.

There is magic waiting to happen; a time has come when many dreams can become real. And there is an urgency, though everything happens in its own time. What does this all mean? For each of us it is different, because it requires that we live our uniqueness. We are being asked to behave as adults who are prepared to take our own destiny and the destiny of the world in both hands. Nothing is certain, but many things will be allowed to happen. When the two worlds come together, when a new link of love is forged through the hearts of the whole of humanity, when the heart of the world opens, the future will be born. And the future has already been born, only we have not noticed it. We are the link of love; we are the heart of the world; we are the future. And yet we still look at the shadows of the past, not recognizing the dawn as it breaks around us.

Why, at this moment of opportunity, have we deserted ourself? At each time of transition the illusions of the last age close tightly around. This is true of our individual journey, which is why the passageway of initiation is so narrow. We have to leave behind that which we consider precious: the attachments of the past have to go. And so they cling to us, not wanting to be discarded, to be left behind. The illusions of a dying age are very dangerous, because they carry the potency of all of our unlived dreams, of everything that was never fulfilled. Are we prepared to give up all of our expectations, everything that we wanted for ourself? Are we prepared to step into the unknown in a state of poverty, expecting nothing? Yet this is the only way one can make such a transition.

There are also forces that stand in the way of this new awakening, that want to keep us in the grip of their power structures, to keep us enslaved with greed and self-centered desires. They have even polluted the spiritual arena, where self-improvement rather than selfless service is encouraged. One cannot sell devotion or market how to give oneself. Love has no power structures or hierarchies. But in the dense patterns of our worldly thought-forms we have forgotten that the real gifts of God, like the sunlight, are always free. For centuries the secrets of divine love and the knowledge of His oneness have been given freely from heart to heart.

This knowledge of love is now being made public, according to the need of the time. The invisible is being made visible and the signs of God are revealing themselves in a new way. If we dare to step out of the patterns of our conditioning, if we want nothing for ourself, then the doorways of love are open to us and there is work to be done. We are the song of the soul of the world. We carry the names of God written in our hearts, and they are waiting to come alive in a new way. In the energy of divine oneness, the opposites have come together, but the energy of oneness needs us to bring this potential into manifestation, to make it part of the fabric of daily life. Without our full participation it will remain just a promise, something that might have happened.

Lovers know how to give themselves to the moment, to be awake in the eternal now. They are not afraid of the consequences of their actions because they know that only His love is real. They honor their soul's pledge to witness His oneness. In the mirror of their heart a secret is being born, and in the network of lovers this secret is coming alive. Humanity has forgotten that the world can only be transformed through love, that love is the greatest power in creation. But His lovers have always known this, and long ago they gave themselves to the work of His love.

Without this central note of pure love, the future will remain just a dream and the patterns of the past will close more tightly around us. With love, joy will return, and joy will cleanse away the pollution of the world, the negative thought-forms and patterns of greed that devour so much of our energy and life force. When joy returns to the hearts and lives of humanity, the whole world will come alive in a new way. The soul of the world will sing the oneness of God and we will know why we are here.

Notes

INTRODUCTION

1. *The Gift*, trans. Daniel Ladinsky, p. 49.

GLOBAL ENERGY PATTERNS

1. *Divine Flashes*, trans. William Chittick and Peter Lamborn Wilson, p. 79.

2. See Sara Sviri, *The Taste of Hidden Things*, pp. 72–73.

3. The ninth-century Sufi al-Hakîm at-Tirmidhî writes of the "forty righteous men": "It is due to them that the denizens of the earth are guarded from affliction; people are protected from misfortunes. Due to them the rain falls and crops grow. None of them ever dies unless God brings forth another to replace him. They never curse anything, they never cause harm to those beneath them, they never regard them with arrogance or contempt; they don't envy those who are above them and they don't have any desire for the world." (*Nawârdir al-usûl*, unpublished translation by Sara Sviri).

4. Claude Addas, *Quest for the Red Sulphur*, p. 151.

5. For example, the plane of unity cannot manifest through a fragmented psyche.

6. *St. Matthew*, 20: 1–16.

7. Interestingly, there are many families in the West in which the relationship between parents and children has shifted towards a greater equality: parents and children relating together on an equal basis as individuals, rather than the older hierarchical model which kept the generations separate.

EVERYDAY LIFE

1. *The Drunken Universe*, trans. Peter Lamborn Wilson and Nasrollah Pourjavady, p. 99.
2. *The Gift*, p. 254.
3. *One-Handed Basket Weaving*, trans. Coleman Barks, p. 14.
4. *St. Matthew*, 9: 17.

THE PLANE OF UNITY

1. "Auguries of Innocence," *The Complete Writings of William Blake*, p. 431.
2. *The Book of Secrets*, trans. from the French by Lynn Finegan, ch. I, ll. 32–35.
3. Shâh Ne'matollâh, *The Drunken Universe*, p. 96.
4. Gharib Nawâz, *The Drunken Universe*, p. 99.
5. In *Dark Wood to White Rose* (p. xv), Helen Luke describes how the journey is imaged in the stages of Dante's *Divine Comedy*, which begins with the *Inferno*:

> ...the journey of one man alone in the fullness of conscious choice down the center of the darkness and beyond to the realization and acceptance of individual responsibility in the Purgatorio. Then, after the long hard climb of self-knowledge is complete, the wayfarer comes to the "happy ending" in the Paradiso, where he glimpses the infinitely varied vision of wholeness....
>
> At the moment of supreme consciousness, which Dante describes in the last canto of his poem... he sees the entire universe in the Center, and finally in a flash of awareness, knows the truth of incarnation—nature, humanity, and God as one.

THE HEART OF THE WORLD

1. *The Divine Comedy*, trans. Dorothy L. Sayers, *Paradiso*, Canto XXXIII, ll. 85–87.
2. Quoted by Bhatnagar, *Dimensions of Classical Sufi Thought*, p. 92.
3. The alchemists understood the connection between the *anima mundi* and the innermost secret of man. The source of the wisdom and knowledge of the all-pervading essence of the *anima mundi* was "the inner-most and most secret numinosum of man" (see C.G. Jung, *Collected Works*, vol. 14, para. 372).
4. This is already being played out on the Internet, with the P2P (peer to peer) programming movement started by Napster, challenging any idea of central control.

SPIRITUAL SECURITY

1. *Atom from the Sun of Knowledge*, trans. Lex Hixon, p. 246.
2. *The Book of Chuang Tzu*, trans. Martin Palmer and Elizabeth Breuilly, p. 23.
3. *Tao Te Ching*, trans. Stephen Mitchell, 80.
4. *Tao Te Ching*, 44.

JOY

1. "Infant Joy," *Songs of Innocence*.
2. "i thank you God for most this amazing day," E. E. Cummings, *Complete Poems: 1904-1962*.
3. Ibn 'Arabî writes in some detail of the "safety in servanthood"; see William Chittick, *The Sufi Path of Knowledge*, pp. 309–331.
4. Ibn 'Arabî, *The Seven Days of the Heart*, trans. Pablo

Beneito and Stephen Hirtenstein, p. 44.
5. Rûmî, *Light upon Light*, trans. Andrew Harvey, p. 163.
6. *Songs of Innocence.*

MAGIC

1. "Burnt Norton," ll. 42–43, *Four Quartets.*
2. *A Midsummer Night's Dream*, IV.I, ll. 203–215.
Bottom is misquoting *I Corinthians*, 2:9: "Eye hath
not seen, nor ear heard, neither have entered into the heart
of man, the things which God hath prepared for those that
love Him."
3. In Sufi symbolism, the orient is the world of light, or the
real home of the soul, while the occident is the world of
matter.

IMAGINATION

1. "A Vision of the Last Judgement," Blake, *Complete Writings*, ed. G. Keynes, p. 606.
2. *Psychological Reflections*, ed. Jolande Jacobi, p. 39.
3. Henry Corbin, *Creative Imagination in the Sufism of Ibn
'Arabî*, p. 189.
4. *Creative Imagination in the Sufism of Ibn 'Arabî*, p. 189.
5. *Plotinus*, trans. A.H. Armstrong, vol. 4, p. 419.
6. E. W. Warren, "Imagination in Plotinus," *Classical
Quarterly* 16, p. 277.

THE CHILDREN OF THE ORIENT

1. "Hymn of Life," *The Vision of the Fool*, ed. Brian Keeble,
p. 33.

Bibliography

Addas, Claude. *Quest for the Red Sulphur*. Cambridge: Islamic Texts Society, 1993.

The Bible, Authorized Version. London: 1611.

Bhatnagar, R.S. *Dimensions of Classical Sufi Thought*. Delhi: Motilal Banarsidass, 1984.

Blake, William. *The Complete Writings of William Blake*. Ed. Geoffrey Keynes. Oxford: Oxford University Press, 1969.

Chittick, William C. *The Sufi Path of Knowledge*. Albany: State University of New York Press, 1989.

Chuang Tzu. *The Book of Chuang Tzu*. Trans. Martin Palmer with Elizabeth Breuilly. London: Arkana, 1996.

Collins, Cecil. *The Vision of the Fool*. Ed. Brian Keeble. Ipswich: Golgomooza Press, 1994.

Corbin, Henry. *Creative Imagination in the Sufism of Ibn 'Arabî*. Princeton: Princeton University Press, 1969.

Cummings, E. E. *Complete Poems: 1904-1962*. Ed. George J. Firmage. New York: Liveright Publishing, 1979.

Dante. *The Divine Comedy*. Trans. Dorothy L. Sayers. Harmonsworth: Penguin Books, 1962.

Eliot, T.S. *Four Quartets*. London: Faber and Faber, 1944.

—. *Collected Poems*. London: Faber and Faber, 1963.

Fakhruddîn 'Irâqî. *Divine Flashes*. Trans. Peter Lamborn Wilson. New York: Paulist Press, 1982.

Hafiz. *The Gift*. Trans. Daniel Ladinsky, New York: Arkana, Penguin Group, 1999.

Hixon, Lex. *Atom from the Sun of Knowledge*. Westport, Connecticut: Pir Publications, 1993.

Ibn 'Arabî. *The Seven Days of the Heart*. Trans. Pablo Beneito and Stephen Hirtenstein. Oxford: Anqa Publishing, 2000.

Jung, C. G. *Collected Works*. London: Routledge & Kegan Paul.

—. *Psychological Reflections*. London: Routledge & Kegan Paul, 1971.

Lao-tsu. *Tao Te Ching*. Trans. Stephen Mitchell. New York: Harper & Row, 1988.

Luke, Helen. *Dark Wood to White Rose*. New York: Parabola Books, 1989.

Plotinus. *Works*. Trans. A.H. Armstrong. London: Heinemann, 1996–1984.

Rûmî. *One-Handed Basket Weaving*. Trans. Coleman Barks. Athens, Georgia: Maypop Books, 1991.

—. *Light Upon Light*. Trans. Andrew Harvey. Berkeley: North Atlantic Books, 1996.

Sviri, Sara. *The Taste of Hidden Things*. Inverness: Golden Sufi Center, 1997.

Wilson, Peter Lamborn and Nasrollah, Pourjavady. *The Drunken Universe*. Grand Rapids: Phanes Press, 1987.

Index

meditation (cont.), 57, 58,
96, 97
merging, 112
Midsummer Night's Dream,
91-92, 145
microcosm, 16, 47, 48, 98
monotheism, 108
Mother Teresa (d. 1997), 29
mundus imaginalis, 113
mystical union, 22

N
Naqshbandi, 63
Nasruddin, 83-84, 96
new age, xiii, xvii, 41, 50, 51,
105, 122
Newtonian physics, 2
non-being, 112, 121

O
opposites, 25, 82, 85, 129,
139, 141
organic structure, 34, 50, 51
orient, 138-139, 145

P
Parsifal, 113
particle physics, 2
patriarchy, 134, 137
patterns of energy, 3, 70, 118,
135
phantasia, 113
plane of unity, 35, 40-42, 142
Plato (d. 348 B.C.), 32, 120
Plotinus (d. 262), 121
pole, 5, 100
power animal, 114
prayer, 41, 58, 66, 82, 86

Prophet, The, 82
purification, 6, 22-23
Puritans, 93

Q
Qur'an, 30, 38, 55, 80, 130

R
remembrance, 47, 63, 76
renunciation, 22
revelation, 26, 27, 37, 38-39,
40, 43, 47, 60, 109, 130,
131, 132
Roman Empire, 13
Rûmî (d. 1273), 29-30, 56

S
samadhi, 11
Sanskrit, 111
security, 8, 28, 57-61, 72-73,
74, 78, 92, 138, 144
spiritual security, 57-58,
138
Self, 6, 58, 64, 66, 111, 112,
114, 122
self-absorption, 9
selfless service, 66, 89, 97, 140
servanthood, 65, 66, 80-81,
82, 144
Shâh Ne'matollâh (d. 1431),
38
Shakespeare (d. 1616), 91, 92-
93
shaman, 92, 97, 114-115
sheikh, 112
signs of God, 59, 140
signs of life, 96, 97, 106
sirr, 101, 102, 103

Acknowledgments

For permission to use copyrighted material, the author gratefully wishes to acknowledge: Penguin Books Ltd., for permission to quote from *The Book of Chuang Tzu*, translations by Martin Palmer and Elizabeth Breuilly, published by Arkana/Penguin Group, London (1996), page 23 of the chapter "The Nurturing of Life"; HarperCollins Publishers Inc., for permission to quote from *Tao Te Ching by Lao Tzu: a New English Version with Foreword and Notes by Stephen Mitchell* (1988); Harcourt, Inc., for permission to quote from *Four Quartets* by T. S. Eliot (1936); Daniel Ladinsky, for permission to quote from *The Gift: Poems of Hafiz, the Great Sufi Master* translated by Daniel Ladinsky (1999); and for permission to quote from *I Heard God Laughing: Renderings of Hafiz* by Daniel Ladinsky (1996); Omega Publications, New Lebanon, NY (www.omega.com), for permission to quote from *The Drunken Universe* by Peter Lamborn Wilson and Nasrollah Pourjavady (1987); Paulist Press, for permission to quote from *Fakhruddîn' Irâqî: Divine Flashes and Early Islamic Mysticism* translated by William Chittick and Peter Lamborn Wilson (1982), used with permission of Paulist Press (www.paulistpress.com); Pir Publications, for permission to quote from *Atom from the Sun of Knowledge* translated by Lex Hixon (1993); Coleman Barks, for permission to quote from *RUMI: One-Handed Basket Weaving* by Coleman Barks, Maypop (1991); Liveright Publishing Corporation, for permission to quote "i thank You God for most this amazing." Copyright 1950, © 1978, 1991 by the Trustees for the E. E. Cummings Trust. Copyright © 1979 by George James Firmage, from *COMPLETE POEMS: 1904-1962* by E. E. Cummings, edited by George J. Firmage.

LLEWELLYN VAUGHAN-LEE, Ph.D., is a Sufi teacher. He has specialized in the area of dreamwork, integrating the ancient Sufi approach to dreams with the insights of modern psychology. Author of several books on the subject, Llewellyn has lectured extensively throughout the United States, Canada, and Europe. He currently lives in California.

THE GOLDEN SUFI CENTER is a California Religious Non-Profit Corporation dedicated to making the teachings of the Naqshbandi Sufi Path available to all seekers. For further information about the activities of the Center and Llewellyn Vaughan-Lee's lectures, please contact us at:

The Golden Sufi Center
P.O. Box 428
Inverness, California 94937

tel: (415) 663-8773
fax: (415) 663-9128
email: goldensufi@aol.com
website: www.goldensufi.org

BY **SARA SVIRI**

THE TASTE OF HIDDEN THINGS
Images of the Sufi Path

～✎

BY **PETER KINGSLEY**

IN THE DARK PLACES OF WISDOM

～✎

A selection of live talks given by Irina Tweedie, Llewellyn Vaughan-Lee, Sara Sviri, and Peter Kingsley are available. Further information is available through our website, or contact us for a free catalog.

～✎